CHESTER HIMES

In the same series:

MODERN LITERATURE MONOGRAPHS

GENERAL EDITOR: Lina Mainiero

CHESTER HIMES

James Lundquist

FREDERICK UNGAR PUBLISHING CO.
NEW YORK

Contents

Chronology

Himes a two-year suspended sentence. Himes is arrested in November and charged with armed robbery. Sentenced to 20–25 years of hard labor at the Ohio State Penitentiary, 27 December.

1934   "Crazy in the Stir" published in *Esquire*, followed by other *Esquire* stories, including "To What Red Hell."

1936   Paroled from Ohio State Penitentiary, May, after serving seven years, five months. Works as waiter, bellhop. Sells short stories to *Esquire* and *Coronet*.

1937   Marries Jean Johnson, 13 August.

1938–41   Works as laborer for Works Progress Administration, then as research assistant in Cleveland Public Library, and is finally assigned to work on a history of Cleveland as part of the Ohio Writer's Project. Works on Louis Bromfield's Malabar Farm near Pleasant Valley, Ohio.

1942   Himes and Jean move to Los Angeles. Works at over 20 jobs in next three years, mostly in the shipyards.

1944   Receives fellowship from Julius Rosenwald Foundation. Moves to New York City.

1945   *If He Hollers Let Him Go* published by Doubleday. Returns to California to live on ranch owned by Jean's brother near Susanville. Works on *Lonely Crusade*.

1946   Returns to New York City.

1947   *Lonely Crusade* published by Knopf.

1948   Lives at Yaddo, the writers' colony at Saratoga Springs, New York, May and June. Delivers talk at the University of Chicago on "The Dilemma of the Negro Writer."

1949   Works at various jobs, mostly as caretaker at resorts, country clubs, and estates.

1950   Continues caretaker jobs; conducts seminar in creative writing at North Carolina College in June.

1951   Works as porter, janitor, and bellhop. Separates from wife.

1952   *Cast the First Stone* published by Coward McCann.

1953   Leaves for Europe, April. Arrives in Paris; there associates with Richard Wright, the expatriate black writer; moves to Arcachon, on the Bay of Biscay, then to London.

1954   Moves to Mallorca. *The Third Generation* published by World.

1955   *The Primitive* published by New American Library; Himes's French publisher Marcel Duhamel suggests Himes write some detective fiction.

1957   *For Love of Imabelle*, first of the Grave Digger and Coffin Ed novels, is published by Fawcett in a paperback original.

1958   Awarded the Grand Prix Policier.

1959   *The Crazy Kill* and *The Real Cool Killers* are published by Berkeley.

1960   *All Shot Up* and *The Big Gold Dream* are published by Berkeley.

1961   *Pinktoes* published by Olympia Press in Paris.

1965   *Cotton Comes to Harlem* published by Putnam.

1966   *The Heat's On* and *Run Man Run* published by Putnam.

1969   Movie version of *Cotton Comes to Harlem* starring Godfrey Cambridge and Sidney Poitier released.

1972   Vol. I of Himes's autobiography, *The Quality of Hurt*, is published by Doubleday.

1973   *Black on Black*; *Baby Sister and Selected Writings* published by Doubleday.

November 1928

"The Negro was invented in America."
—*John Oliver Killens,*
"The Black Writer Vis-À-Vis His Country"

In November 1928, Chester Himes was arrested in Chicago for armed robbery. At the detective bureau his feet were bound, his wrists were handcuffed behind his back, and he was hung upside down on an open door and pistol-whipped until he confessed. A few days earlier he had heard a chauffeur in Bunch Boy's gambling club on Cedar Avenue in Cleveland bragging about the cash his employer kept in his house on Cedar Hill. Himes entered the house Thanksgiving eve, pulled out a .44-caliber revolver, and took more than $20,000 in cash and $28,000 in jewelry from the terrified occupants. He fled by train to Chicago and checked into a hotel on the South Side. When he tried to fence some of the jewelry at a pawnshop near the Loop, the pawnbroker called the police. Himes was delivered to the Cuyahoga County Jail in Cleveland. On 27 December 1928, he was sentenced to twenty to twenty-five years of hard labor at the Ohio State Penitentiary.[1]

Himes was nineteen when he went into the penitentiary; he was twenty-six when he came out. He

1

survived his prison years partly because of his capacity for anger and rage, but mostly because he learned to articulate that anger through writing. His distinctive kind of fiction has at one time or another offended the sensibilities of blacks, whites, communists, right-wingers, and critics of all denominations. This is a response to a vision, described by Himes himself, as "the fear that inhabits the minds of all blacks who live in America, and the various impacts on this fear precipitated by communism, industrialism, unionism, the war, white women, and marriage within the race."[2] Himes's education in that fear began early, continued long, and led to an objectification of evil and injustice found nowhere else in the American novel.

Himes, with his taut, upbeat prose, is more than a master stylist. Through a career that spans four decades, Himes moved toward the mastery of four distinct types of novel in a way that distinguishes him as one of the most versatile as well as one of the most enigmatic of modern writers. Himes's novels are not for the timid; they are bitter, structured around scenes of pervasive unpleasantness, rely heavily upon the symbolic implications of nightmares, and are filled with violence: fists crunch into jawbones, ballpeen hammers drop like weighted darkness, switchblade knives click open, pistols blast flame into the Harlem night, and murdered men lie sprawled among the cigarette wrappers and broken glass on the ghetto sidewalks. But this is not violence for the sake of morbid thrills only; it is based on Himes's conviction—arrived at in prison, expressed in all of his books, and reinforced by a hundred turns of plot—that people will do anything. The result is a singular kind of tension: reading a Himes novel is like standing on an electric grid, blindfolded, waiting for the current to be turned on, and knowing that it will be. Reading Himes is also an

education in social history by a master of mayhem
who specializes in powerfully individualized portraits
of black men literally being driven crazy by white
society and themselves. Himes gives us a vision of a
racially obsessed and decadent America. But more
important than that picture—as terrifying as it is—is
his ability to coolly achieve, in his best work, an effective union of social protest and art.

Himes was born on 29 July 1909 in Jefferson City,
Missouri. His father, Joseph Sandy Himes, who taught
blacksmithing and wheelwrighting, headed the me-
chanical-arts department at Lincoln Institute, now
Lincoln University. Chester was the youngest in his
family, with two older brothers, Joseph and Edward.
His mother, light-skinned and proud, claimed that her
family, the Bomars, were descended from English nobility. This claim, along with her aristocratic attitudes,
was a lasting source of conflict between her and her
husband.

By 1917 Professor Himes was on the faculty of
Alcorn A.&M. College in Mississippi. Buying a car,
he earned the uneasy distinction, as a black man, of
being the only automobile owner in the county. He got
into trouble with white farmers in the area because
they claimed the car frightened their mules, and he
was fired from his job.

In 1921 Professor Himes got another position at
Branch Normal College in Pine Bluff, Arkansas. Chester and Joe were enrolled in first-year courses even
though Chester was only a youngster. Near the end of
the term in 1922, when students were asked to display
special skills or techniques in an auditorium before
their parents, Joe and Chester were asked to give a
chemistry demonstration. They decided to make a tor-
pedo from saltpeter, charcoal, and ground glass. But
because Chester had disobeyed his mother, she would

not let him perform. When Joe mixed the contents together, they exploded, blinding him. He was rushed to the white hospital and was refused admittance. At the black hospital, his parents were told nothing could be done. For Chester Himes, the "quality of hurt," which he uses as the title of his autobiography was suddenly real. Five days later, his mother took Joe to Barnes Hospital in St. Louis.

In the fall of 1922 Chester's father moved the family to St. Louis. Despite his abilities, Professor Himes had to take a job as a waiter in a beer hall. Chester was enrolled at Wendell Philips High School, where he was lonely and friendless, and where he received his first taste of the violent environment he was to occupy through much of his life. In schoolyard fights, his right shoulder blade (which never healed properly) was broken, his teeth chipped, and his left ear almost ripped from his head.

In 1923 his father next moved the family, including Joe, to Cleveland, where two of Professor Himes's sisters and a brother lived. But work opportunities were not much better than in St. Louis, and the Himeses were forced to live at first with relatives with whom Mrs. Himes did not get along. Professor Himes eventually found work as a carpenter, and was able to buy a house in the Glenville neighborhood, then mainly a middle-class area. Chester graduated from Glenville High School in January 1926.

He planned to attend Ohio State University in the fall, but in the meantime took a job as busboy in the Wade Park Hotel. One day, after several weeks at the hotel, he fell down the shaft of a service elevator, breaking his jaw, his left arm, and three vertebrae. In a grim repetition of what his brother Joe had experienced, he was turned away from the new white hospital on 105th Street and was taken instead to the

Huron Road Hospital on Euclid Avenue. His recovery
was slow, and when he came out of the hospital he
had to wear an awkward brace, but the Ohio State
Industrial Commission paid his expenses and put him
on a $75 monthly disability pension. The hotel, be-
cause it was liable, agreed to continue his salary (in-
vestigators concluded that the hotel was at fault because the stationary doors had failed to lock
automatically). A lawsuit could have been initiated,
but Himes's father suggested taking the pension and
signing waivers. This led to another disagreement between Himes's parents, a disagreement that was further
complicated when Mrs. Himes went to the hotel and
angrily told the hotel officials that they had taken advantage of her son. They responded by cutting off
Chester's salary. Since the waivers had been signed,
there was nothing the family could do.

Himes nonetheless entered Ohio State University
in September. He bought a raccoon coat, a pipe, and a
Model T roadster, and pledged Alpha Phi Alpha fraternity. For awhile he fell eagerly into college life,
puffing on the pipe, driving the roadster, and even
helping to pull down the stadium gates at the Ohio
State-Michigan State game that fall. But his injury
continued to bother him, he was suffering from depression, and he did badly in his classes that first
quarter.

When he returned to school for the winter term,
he began to become increasingly disturbed by the way
he and other black students were trying to imitate
white behavior. This discontentment led him, after a
formal dance during spring quarter, to take some
friends to a combination speakeasy-whorehouse without telling them the truth about what it was. One of
the prostitutes recognized him, became jealous, and
started screaming obscenities at the college girls. A

fight broke out, the incident was reported to the dean of men, and Himes was asked to leave school.

Himes, still sick and depressed, returned to Cleveland. During the summer, he began hanging around Bunch Boy's gambling club, playing blackjack poker. He soon attracted the attention of Bunch Boy himself, who reputedly had connections with the Capone organization. Himes was caught up in the hustling life and went to work at the Gilsy, a notorious prostitution hotel, as a bellhop, making $50 and more a night. He shot dice at Hotstuff's across the street, and, as Himes himself testifies, met some of the bizarre characters who later were to show up in his detective stories.[3]

He bought expensive clothes, a second-hand Nash (which he smashed into a concrete stanchion), associated with a small-time thief named Benny, smoked opium, and stole cars. He also met his first wife, Jean Johnson, and with her started to run a whiskey joint in an alley back of Bunch Boy's. Benny talked him into burglarizing the Y.M.C.A. building on Cedar Avenue, where the Ohio National Guard had stored some arms and ammunition. Himes and Benny stole a case of .45-caliber automatics and some boxes of cartridges, hoping to sell the pistols to steel workers in Warren and Youngstown. The next night the two were arrested. Himes's mother pleaded for him and the judge gave him a suspended sentence; Benny received thirty days. When Benny was released, he and Himes stole a car and drove to Columbus. There Himes picked up a mislaid student identity card and used it to write bad checks all over Columbus. He was caught and this time his father did the arguing with the judge, succeeding in getting Himes a two-year suspended sentence and a five-year bench parole. A month later he was arrested in Chicago for the Thanksgiving-eve robbery that sent him to prison.

Himes was well prepared for prison life. His gambling experience enabled him to move easily within the prison walls, where much of the power and much of the prestige among inmates depended on gambling operations. (He was still receiving pension checks.) Nonetheless, Himes always carried a knife, because the Ohio State Penitentiary was a place where he saw convicts killed in arguments over geography (whether Paris is in France or France is in Paris) and for not passing food to someone else at the table. He also saw a strange form of heroism in the Easter Monday fire of 1930, when many of the convicts who had escaped to the prison yard struggled to get back into the cellblocks to rescue other prisoners who were trapped there. Despite the display of courage, over three hundred thirty men burned to death in their cells.

Writing, if it does not exactly flourish inside a prison, is a major diversion for many inmates, and it is not surprising that Himes should have started to write stories while in the penitentiary. What is surprising, however, is the rapidity of his success. He was first published in black weekly newspapers and magazines —the Atlanta *World*, the Pittsburgh *Courier*, the *Afro American*, the *Bronzeman*, and *Abbott's Monthly*. And then, in 1934, his short story, "Crazy in the Stir" (the only byline being his prison number), was published in *Esquire*.

His stories—"Crazy in the Stir," "To What Red Hell" (about the Easter Monday fire), "The Visiting Hour," "Every Opportunity," "The Night's for Crying," and "Strictly Business"—deal with prison life, with crimes and with criminals, and they center on the anger, fear, and pain that is to be found in his later writing. They also bear testimony to what Himes had learned since the steel doors slid shut behind him in

1928. "It is nonsense, even falsehood, to say that serving seven and a half years in one of the most violent prisons on earth will have no effect on a human being," Himes writes in *The Quality of Hurt*. "But as far as I could determine at the time, and for a long time afterward, the only effect it had on me was to convince me that people will do anything—white people, black people, all people. Why should I be surprised when white men cut out some poor black man's nuts, or when black men eat the tasty palms of white explorers?"[4]

It is Himes's conviction that people will do anything that distinguishes his first writing and that accounts both for the level of violence and the often abrupt shifts in plot that occur in his novels. The reader of Himes must be prepared for sudden desperate acts on the part of Himes's characters and must also realize that unsuspected consequences may wait on the next page. Himes's conception of the erratic nature of human personality opens up to him possibilities in every story that sometime become unnerving but are always redeemed by surprise.

Continuing as a writer was difficult when Himes was paroled to his mother in 1936. His disability pension had stopped, and he began to drift into his old life, whoring, getting high on marijuana, and hanging around other ex-convicts. In desperation his mother had him paroled to his father, who was working as a Works Progress Administration (WPA) teacher in Cleveland. The change made a difference. Himes married Jean, worked as a waiter in a country club and then as a bellhop in several hotels, and managed to sell some short stories to *Esquire* and *Coronet*. He worked for the WPA as a laborer for a time, became a research assistant in the Cleveland Library, and finally became part of the Ohio Writers' Project (he was assigned to work on a history of Cleveland).

But with the start of American involvement in World War II, the WPA programs stopped and Himes was out of work. He tried to find employment at the factories in Cleveland that were cranking up for the war effort but was unsuccessful. He applied through his parole officer for restoration of his citizenship so he could leave Cleveland, and got it. He went to Pleasant Valley, Ohio, where he worked on Malabar Farm, the thousand-acre tract owned by the novelist and agrarian romantic Louis Bromfield, who had won a Pulitzer Prize for *Early Autumn* in 1926. Bromfield read the novel about prison life Himes had been working on, *Black Sheep*, and offered to help him find a publisher. But even with Bromfield's help, Himes was not able to persuade an editor to take the book. Himes soon became discontented at Malabar, realizing that he was only hiding from the racial tensions that were becoming central to his work, and he and Jean took a Greyhound bus to Los Angeles.

It was in Los Angeles that Himes experienced the anger, frustration, and sense of rejection that, combined with his prison experiences, produced the vision of American life that emerges in *If He Hollers Let Him Go* and *Lonely Crusade*, his first published novels. "Los Angeles hurt me racially as much as any city I have ever known—much more than any city I remember from the South," Himes has recalled.[5] Langston Hughes had given Himes a list of people to see in Hollywood, and Himes had some hope of finding work as a screenwriter. Bromfield had gone to California to work on the screen version of Hemingway's *For Whom the Bell Tolls*, and had taken Himes's book along to show to some producers, but nothing came of either the list or the producers. Himes soon learned that "Los Angeles was a very prejudiced place and the only jobs black people had were in the kitchens in Hollywood and Beverly Hills."[6] He even discovered that the black people in the cast of *Cabin in the Sky* were jim-crowed in the MGM commissary.[7] So Himes went to work in the shipyards, and he had twenty-three jobs during the first three years of the war. Out of all those jobs and despite the mechanical training he had picked up from his father, Himes had only two that involved skilled work—as apprentice shipfitter in Kaiser's Shipyard No. 1 in Richmond and as a shipwright's helper in the Los Angeles Shipyard at San Pedro Harbor.

His time in the shipyards, as bitter as it was, gave him the setting for *If He Hollers Let Him Go*, which was accepted for publication by Doubleday, Doran, and Company in 1944, the same year Himes was awarded a fellowship from the Julius Rosenwald Foundation. Himes was able to leave Los Angeles and move to New York City. But he was hurt by his inability to support his wife the way he wanted to and was angered by his racial experience on the west coast. He fell into a routine of sex and drinking that led his wife, when she saw what he was doing, to attempt suicide. Jean's desperation shocked Himes into pulling himself together.

If He Hollers Let Him Go received good reviews in 1945, although some critics picked up on the objections that were to follow Himes throughout his later books: objections to the abrupt, almost melodramatic turns of plot, to the erratic behavior of the novel's hero, to the bitter tone of the book, to Himes's failure to point out a solution to the racial problems he raises, and to the general unpleasantness of the narrative. One of the most typical, as well as one of the most positive, reviews was written by W. S. Lynch in the November 17th issue of the *Saturday Review of Literature*: "Gall and wormwood have gone into this book, the bitterest we have come across in a long time. Ches-

ter B. Himes . . . has written a short novel of racial
protest as hair-raising as a shriek in the dark. And
snuggling deeper under the blankets will not stop the
piercing reverberations. . . . This book is another cry
out of the depths."[8]

Despite the reception the novel received, it did
not win the $2500 Doubleday, Doran-George Wash-
ington Carver Award for which it was considered.
When an insipid novel called *Mrs. Palmer's Honey*, by
Fannie Cook, was awarded the prize money, Himes
was infuriated, and went after the critics in "The Author Talks Back" feature in the *Saturday Review*. He
defended his use of objectionable language, and then
asked why—given the immense flexibility and power
the United States had demonstrated in the war effort
—when it came to solving a critical problem of another sort, such as the condition of black people in
America, incidental writers like him were supposed to
come up with the solution.[9] Himes's disappointment
with certain aspects of the reaction to his book as well
as with his publisher's handling of it led him, through
the intercession of Carl Van Vechten, novelist, photog-
rapher, and music critic, to switch to Knopf for his
next novel.

To write that next book, which would turn out to
be *Lonely Crusade*, Himes decided to return to California and live in a three-room shack on a ranch
owned by Jean's brother on Honey Lake along U. S.
Highway 395 about seventy-five miles north of Reno.
The driving trip west was terrifying. Himes and Jean
had difficulty getting served anywhere they stopped,
and they traveled with a loaded rifle from Illinois on.
The shack turned out to be full of sand lizards, and the
nearest town where groceries and supplies could be
obtained was Susanville, seventeen miles away; but
Himes fixed the little house up and managed to write

the first draft of *Lonely Crusade* there. In 1946 he returned to New York and finished the novel in a garage apartment at Wading River on Long Island.

The book went to press even though some people in the editorial department were worrying that at least one of the characterizations in the novel was so strongly realistic that a libel suit might result. As it turned out, libel was the least of Himes's problems when *Lonely Crusade* appeared on 8 October 1947. Blanche Knopf had lined up radio appearances for Himes. He was also to appear before the book department at Macy's and Bloomingdale's the day of publication. Himes's father had even traveled from Cleveland for the big day. But when Himes went to Macy's, the head of the book department stopped him and guiltily said, "Well, we're going to stop this procedure of having authors speak to the booksellers because that would show favoritism since we couldn't do it for all the authors."[10] Himes next went to Bloomingdale's. No copies of the book were on display, and the manager of the book department would not even see him. When he got home to pick up Jean to go to the Mary McBride radio program, he found a telegram informing him that his appearance had been canceled. Later in the day he learned that he had also been dropped from the CBS network show, on which he had been scheduled to appear.

What had happened to make *Lonely Crusade* so suddenly unacceptable? As Himes interpreted it, the abrupt reversal is to be attributed to the activity of the Communist Party—this all occurred at a time when the party, though diminished, still had some influence. A cartoon in *The Daily Worker* showed Himes walking across the page carrying a white flag. Himes's unsympathetic portrayal of communists in the black community and in the labor movement is what caused the greatest irritation. But he had also rejected the party-line solution to the racial problem in the United States, a solution patterned on Lenin's answer to "the national question" (that blacks in the United States are a separate nation, that they should have self-determination, and that therefore a Negro Soviet Republic should be formed in the South).[11] However, the communists were not alone in rejecting the book. Negative reviews appeared in the *Atlantic Monthly*, in *Commentary*, and in *Ebony*.

After the publication of *Lonely Crusade*, Himes found himself in a position that few other American novelists have occupied. He was being assaulted by communists, fascists, white racists, black racists, and practically every reviewer within those extremes. Again the familiar criticism of Himes's use of melodrama and excessive violence both in scene and language appeared, but he was also denounced for an ugly narrative, confused thematic structure and philosophical dialogue, and too limited an outlook. The antagonism of black critics was especially strong. In an angry interview years later with the novelist John A. Williams, Himes analyzed the novel's reception. "I know why the black people disliked the book—because they're doing the same thing now that I said at that time was necessary," Himes related. "I had the black protagonist, Lee Gordon, a CIO organizer, say that the black man in America needed more than just a superficial state of equality; he needed special consideration because he was so far behind. That you can't just throw him out there and say, 'Give Negroes rights,' because it wouldn't work that way. And so this is what most of the black writers had against it; in saying that, of course, by pleading for special privileges for the black people I was calling them inferior."[12] Even though Himes's point eventually achieved considerable acceptance, 1947 apparently was not the time to make the kind of argument outlined in *Lonely Crusade*.

Himes had received a $2,000 advance for a book that was to be based on his observations in Hollywood during the war and tentatively titled *Immortal Mammy*. But for the next five years after the rejection of *Lonely Crusade*, he found writing to be nearly impossible. He worked as a dishwasher, a janitor, and even shoveled snow. Spending May and June at Yaddo, the writer's colony in Saratoga Springs, was no help. He was able to state his problem, however, in a speech he delivered at the University of Chicago that summer on "The Dilemma of the Negro Novelist in the United States," later printed in Williams's anthology *Beyond the Angry Black*.[13] This statement is not only a piece of unmerciful self-analysis on Himes's own part, it is also a clear statement of his attitude toward the special problems faced by the black writer and an uncompromising justification of the type of novel he had written in *If He Hollers Let Him Go* and *Lonely Crusade*.

Himes said that the black man writing in America must deal with three conflicts involving himself, his environment, and his public. First, if he is to be honest in revealing the truth of his experience, he will find that it is self-degrading to tell the truth about the oppression he has suffered. In writing about the horrors he has experienced, in describing the hurts he has suffered, he will be opening old wounds—an agony much greater than most nonblacks realize. And his reward for all this is to "be reviled by . . . Negroes and whites alike."[14] He will be tempted to tone down the raw statement of his suffering by rationalizing that it is necessary to overcome his race consciousness because his problem is actually the human problem, not simply and exclusively a consequence of being black. Or he may have the urge to look to African culture for an explanation of what he is and how he got that way. "But he will find that he cannot accomplish this departure because he is an American," Himes said. "He will realize in the end that he possesses this heritage of slavery; he is a product of this American culture; his thoughts and emotions and reactions have been fashioned by his American environment. He will discover that he cannot free himself of race consciousness because he cannot free himself of race; that is his motive in attempting to run away. But, to paraphrase a statement of Joe Louis's, 'He may run, but he can't hide.' "[15]

Resolving the personal struggle with his own honesty leads to the next problem for the black writer. He will quickly learn that his American environment places several obstacles between what he wants to write and how it shall eventually appear in print. For one thing, most publishers are reluctant to publish uncompromisingly bitter novels by black writers because such novels are not considered good commercial ventures. If the writer does manage to interest a publisher, he may run into further difficulty with editors whose understanding of the black experience is based almost entirely upon acquaintances with black people who are conventionally educated and financially successful. The editors may then conclude that the honest black writer is psychotic or that his novels deal in a kind of sickness that is greatly exaggerated through the author's paranoid imagination. Such an editor "does not realize that his own reasoning is self-contradictory; that any American Negro's racial experiences, be they psychotic or not, are typical of all Negroes' racial experiences for the simple reason that the source is not the Negro but oppression."[16]

Once his work is published, if it is published the

way the writer wrote it, the public reaction, especially from the black middle class, is likely to be one of hatred and antagonism. Many American blacks, according to Himes, do not want the extent of their collective injuries known because such knowledge makes it more difficult for them to play the American game of success. "The American Negro, we must remember, is an American," Himes stated; "the face may be the face of Africa, but the heart has the beat of Wall Street."[17] The reaction of his white readers is, of course, more expected. When the black writer reveals the scars he bears, it is an affront to the white reader and a reminder of his heritage of guilt. He fears that he will be forced to come to some sort of resolution concerning a history which is as much a part of his consciousness as is slavery a part of the black man's consciousness. The problem the white liberal must face is the reality of the black man's unrelenting hatred for the white race —even worse, the reality that blacks hate white people far more than whites (despite evidence of slave ships, chains, jim crow ordinances, the Ku Klux Klan, and all of it) hate blacks. "To hate white people is one of the first emotions an American Negro develops when he becomes old enough to learn what his status is in American society," Himes explained. "He must, of necessity, hate white people. He would not be—and it would not be human if he did not—develop a hatred for his oppressors. At some time in the lives of every American Negro there has been this hatred for white people; there are no exceptions. It could not possibly be otherwise."[18] So the reactions of readers, both black and white, who prefer to think otherwise must be anticipated by the writer. He must be prepared for the reception Himes received at Macy's and Bloomingdale's the morning *Lonely Crusade* was published.

The hatred that a black writer must deal with

presents a further problem, however. Hatred of his oppressor is an indication of fear, and the black writer consequently finds that he hates himself for being afraid. It is this fear that the writer must reveal, no matter how much it hurts to do so, because until it is revealed and understood there will be little understanding of the other problems—crime, sexuality, family dissolution, religion, ghettoes. In writing about this fear, the black experience may be presented in a way that is repulsive to most readers of both races. But, as Himes stressed in a pronouncement that is a straightforward defense of his own work, "If this plumbing for the truth reveals within the Negro personality homicidal mania, lust for white women, a pathetic sense of inferiority, paradoxical anti-Semitism, arrogance, Uncle Tomism, hate and fear and self-hate, this then is the effect of oppression on the human personality. These are the daily horrors, the daily realities, the daily experiences of an oppressed minority."[19] The open discussion of any such aspects of the black personality would be enough (and certainly it was in 1947) to arouse controversy; that Himes dealt with all of them in a single book is enough to explain the uproar he listened to after *Lonely Crusade* came out. He had portrayed American blacks as soul-sick after centuries of oppression, and he believed that only if this truth, honestly expressed, is faced and accepted, can the kind of growth take place that will move from racial hatred to the hatred of evil itself.

Himes's mainly white audience at the University of Chicago responded with silence, a silence that became part of his life for the next few years. He stayed on in Chicago for a week and drank; he returned to Yaddo and spent the remainder of his time there in an alcoholic fog. When he left Yaddo, he got a job as a caretaker at a summer resort in New Jersey while he

worked on a stage adaptation of *If He Hollers Let
Him Go* that came to nothing. He next worked as a
bellhop and janitor at a Jewish resort in Sullivan
County and then as caretaker at the Copake Country
Club on Lake Copake. In the summer of 1949 he and
Jean moved to Bridgeport, Connecticut, where he
tried to write until the middle of July, when the
money they had saved was nearly gone. To finance a
move to New York City, where Jean was confident she
could get a job with the Welfare Department, Himes
put a classified ad in the paper to sell their fifteen-year-
old Plymouth sedan for $100. What promised to be a
simple and ordinary transaction took an abrupt twist
not unlike the sudden nightmarish turn of plot in a
Himes novel.

Himes sold the car to a young factory worker before noon the day the ad ran, and the buyer promised
to return with the full payment later that afternoon.
Jean had taken all but fifty cents of their remaining
money and had gone to New York City to apply for
her job. Himes decided to drive the Plymouth one last
time to buy some cigarettes. When he pulled out from
his parking place on the way back, his front bumper
pulled off the fender of a new Buick Roadmaster being
driven on the wrong side of the street by an expen-
sively dressed white woman. He could smell cocktails
on her breath when she got out of her car and he
thought that the responsibility for the accident would
be evident to the police. But the officer who arrived
arrested Himes for reckless driving. At the police station the desk sergeant set bail at $25. Himes suggested
that since he was a well-known writer he be released
on his own recognizance. The desk sergeant said no.
Himes would be allowed, however, to call Jean at
eight o'clock that night, when she would be back from
New York. The evening guard shift was not notified of

the sergeant's instructions and Himes was not permitted to use the telephone. The hearing was to be the next day, but was postponed for a week because the driver of the Buick was unable to appear. At eleven o'clock that morning, Himes was allowed to make his call. Jean had remained in the city overnight and was just entering the house as the telephone stopped ringing. She started calling the hospitals to find out if Himes had been injured, and then she called the police.

Himes in the meantime had called Jean's brother Andrew in Baltimore who said he would send $100 to the jail by wire. Himes was taken to the county prison, where he was fingerprinted, photographed, and issued a numbered uniform. Jean arrived at the prison to find out that she could not see her husband because it was Wednesday and visits were allowed only on Tuesday and Thursday. When she returned home, she learned, through a telegram from her brother, about the $100. At the jail they told her that the money had been sent back to the telegraph office. At the telegraph office she was told that she could not have the money because it was addressed to Himes. To obtain it she would have to get a statement signed by both her husband and the warden. The warden told her that it was illegal for prisoners to receive money that way; but when she started to cry, the warden reluctantly agreed to break the rules, and Himes was bailed out. The factory worker got the car for $25 less, and at eight o'clock Thursday morning Himes and Jean were on the train out of Bridgeport.

The accident, the arrest, the county prison, the whole tangled incident left Himes jangled in spirit. "It wasn't that it hurt so much," he remembers. "Nor was I surprised. I believed that the American white man— in fact all Americans, black or white—was capable of

anything. It was just that it stirred up my anxiety,
which had gradually settled down somewhat. It
scrambled the continuity of my memories, probably of
my thoughts also. That is practically the last thing I
remember about the United States in such vivid detail.
I wish it weren't so. It's a tragedy, but my own, however, just my own."[20] Himes had already decided to
leave the United States for Europe if he could; Bridgeport confirmed the decision for him.

Himes and Jean lived in Harlem for a short time
and then moved to a farm owned by a Madison Avenue lawyer near Stamford, Connecticut. Their duties
consisted of minor caretaking and cooking meals on
weekends when the lawyer and his family came out to
the farm. Himes had, in the meantime, shortened his
prison novel and changed the protagonist into a white
man from Mississippi in the hope of getting it accepted by Holt. The next June he conducted a two-
week seminar in creative writing at North Carolina
College in Durham, where his brother Joe, despite his
blindness, was a professor of sociology (he had taken
his Ph.D. at Ohio State University). While in Durham,
Himes received a letter from an editor at Holt that led
him to think *Black Sheep* had been accepted for publication, so when he got back to New York he cele-
brated with a party for his friends at the Theresa
Hotel. But he found out the next day when he showed
up at Holt's office to sign the contract and pick up his
advance that the manuscript was waiting for him in
package form instead. The managing editor had
backed down and the directors of the company had
supported him. After settling the bill at the hotel,
Himes had only a few dollars left.

Another period of frequent moves and equally
frequent jobs began for Himes. He and Jean lived in
Westlake, Vermont, with a California friend and

writer William Gardner Smith (*Anger at Innocence*),
until late fall when Jean became recreational director
of the Women's Reformatory at Mount Kisco, New
York. He lasted one day typing metal stencils for the
addressograph machines at the *Reader's Digest* offices
in Pleasantville, New York (he had tried unsuccess-
fully to get a job on the editorial staff). For the next
three months he worked as a porter and janitor at the
White Plains YMCA, and then he moved back to Harlem and took a room on Convent Avenue, thinking he
had failed as both a writer and a husband. Next came
a job bellhopping at the New Prospect Hotel in Sullivan County.

When he had been staying with his brother Joe in
Durham for the writer's workshop, Himes had read
through parts of a narrative his mother had put together concerning her family history. He combined
some of his mother's notes with his own memories and
put together an autobiographical novel, *The Third
Generation*. The novel, along with *Black Sheep*, was
being passed from publisher to publisher, and Himes
had almost stopped thinking about it when, one day
while filling in at the hotel switchboard, he received a
telegram informing him that World had accepted *The
Third Generation* and that a $2,000 advance was wait-
ing for him.

Himes picked up his money and began the eigh-
teen-month affair with Vandi Haygood (who was then
working as an executive for the International Institute
of Education) that later served as the basis for *The
Primitive*. By Christmas 1952 most of the advance
money was gone, and Himes went north to Bill Smith's
for the winter. When he learned that his agent Margot
Johnson had sold the prison novel, now titled *Cast the
First Stone* to Coward McCann and that he would get
a $1200 advance, Himes decided to make good on the

promise he had made to himself after the Bridgeport
incident to go to Europe. His decision was made easier
when he found out that *Lonely Crusade* had been
cited by French critics as one of the five best American
books published in France in 1952. He booked passage
in February for an April sailing, his departure bright-
ened by the news that he had a $5,000 advance com-
ing from New American Library for reprint rights to
The Third Generation.

"I just wanted out from the United States, that
was all," Himes stated. "I had had it."[21] He left feeling that he had paid his dues and that it was time for
another kind of life. His marriage to Jean was finished,
he had for the first time enough money so that he did
not have to worry about returning to his old life as a
porter or caretaker, and even though he was not finished with *The Primitive*, he had worked through the
agony that thematically dominates his first phase as a
novelist.

But with an abruptness that is again suggestive of
the changes that occur in his fiction, Himes became a
different kind of writer, moving away from the semi-
autobiographical tough-guy novels which show a
touch of the same kind of proletarian influence as do
the novels of Richard Wright, and toward a new genre
—the black detective novel.

The change that took place in Himes showed up
not long after he arrived in Paris. Wright helped him
find a room in the Hôtel Scandinavie on the rue de
Tournon. Through Wright, Himes met James Baldwin
and other black writers and artists who were living in
Paris. But Himes soon tired of this life and in early
summer went to Arcachon, on the Bay of Biscay. He
realized that he had not gotten along well with most of
the people he had met in Paris, perhaps because he
had wearied of talking about misfortune, especially his

own. "At times my soul brothers embarrassed me," he later wrote, "Bragging about their scars, their poor upbringing, and their unhappy childhood. . . . It was a new variety of Uncle-Tomming, a modern version."[22] He was able to finish *The Primitive* as he moved during the next year to London, Mallorca, Terreno, back to Arcachon, and in and out of Paris. But when he received at Terreno the collection of short stories World was to publish as *Black Boogie Woogie*, he was so disgusted with them that he threw them into the sea.

The four novels Himes published after *Lonely Crusade* had received generally good reviews and his reputation was growing in Europe. But the big money had simply not materialized, and in the United States he was in the ominous position of being remembered for his first two books. So it was fortunate when, in 1955, his French publisher Marcel Duhamel suggested that Himes write a detective novel. Not only was Himes ready to try a new direction, he was superbly qualified for it with his early experiences hanging around Bunch Boy's in Cleveland, his recollections of the men he had met while in prison, and, more important, the ability to write the kind of taut narrative with its undercurrent of violence that the detective novel demands.

In *For Love of Imabelle*, the first of the Grave Digger and Coffin Ed novels published by Duhamel, a number of things came together for Himes. First, his imagination was suddenly and somewhat strangely freed from the burden of autobiography that had, despite the power of his earlier novels, made his range seem limited and his quick-action prose occasionally out of place. Second, in the invention of his black detectives, he hit upon two characterizations that are far more memorable than any of his previous protagonists. Third, he discovered in the genre of the detective novel, which thrives on suspicion, fear, and violence, an effective medium for analyzing life and death in the inner city, where Grave Digger and Coffin Ed are not the only ones to be confronted daily with pimps, burglars, junkies, bookmakers, and angry men with pistols. And fourth, the sense of injustice that led him to abandon the United States is at least partially resolved through the unrelenting work of his central characters in balancing evil accounts. Grave Digger and Coffin Ed straighten out much that had only frustrated Himes himself and many of his readers.

In writing his detective novels, Himes accomplished an unusual transition for a writer whose work until he was nearly fifty years old resembles, despite some distinct qualities, the protest writing of so many of his black contemporaries. He also brought his name back into public view when *For Love of Imabelle* won the Grand Prix Policier in 1958, and when *Cotton Comes to Harlem* appeared in a movie version in 1969. Except for relatively short visits to the United States, Himes has continued to live in Europe where his continuing analysis of American life (through a type of novel he deserves primary credit for inventing) has continued to bring him international attention despite many objections to his vicious conception of the black ghetto and his ungenerous view of human nature.

The fear, hurt, and anger that are with Himes from the beginning of his career have thus become transformed and intensified as they became more objective in his work. He begins by writing about himself and the evil and injustice he witnessed in the Ohio State Penitentiary, in the California shipyards, and in the manic-depressive world of the marginally successful novelist. He then shifts to an objectified vision in which the pain he has known as a black man becomes externalized and even universalized through the inner city of his bitterly efficient detectives who are at once the personifications of the racial problem in the United States and a commentary on its solution, if there indeed is one.

Two War Novels

"If he is caught, it is thought he will be lynched."
—*Theodore Dreiser*, "Nigger Jeff"

Robert Bone has made the point that the work of
Himes's generation of writers is marked by the two
great catastrophes they lived through—the great depression and World War II. "They were not," Bone
emphasizes, "like the writers of the 1920s, simply a
lost generation; they were two-time losers, and their
double catastrophe left a characteristic imprint on
their work."[1] The first impulse of most of these writers
who began turning out their first work in the mid-1930s
was social protest, stories and novels with a distinctly
proletarian slant. Himes's early documentary accounts
of prison life are an example, although the protest is
all in the representation, not in any kind of social solution. Another example was provided at the end of the
decade in *Native Son* that became all but overwhelming; Wright provided both a model form of naturalism
and an idiom that sparked imitation after imitation,
which was itself an indication of a problem: *Native Son*
was undoubtedly an inspiration, but it had to be gotten
around. The war experience itself was a help in this
respect partly because it interrupted the work of some
of Wright's imitators and partly because it opened the

discussion of racial oppression in an unexpected way. The war was ostensibly directed against the racist ideas of Hitler, and, by a logical extension, against the entire notion of white supremacy. A new era in American race relations thus seemed inevitable. But there remained a generation of black writers whose work to some critics when it appeared after World War II seemed anachronistic.

These writers, known for a time as the Wright school of urban realists, include, in addition to Himes, Ann Petry (*The Street*, 1946), Curtis Lucas (*Third Ward Newark*, 1946), Willard Savoy (*Alien Land*, 1949), Philip B. Kaye (*Taffy*, 1950), and Lloyd Brown (*Iron City*, 1951). Like Wright, these writers generally view literature as emotional catharsis—as a way of getting rid of inner racial tensions. Because their material so impinges on their consciousness, their novels often have no more form or thematic content than does an extended cry of anguish. Their style is unalleviated brutal realism and their characterization is sociological. As a main theme, they share the idea that the caste system breeds grotesques. And the purpose of much of their writing is to make white readers feel responsible for the protagonist and alter their racist attitudes.[2]

But Himes, as his first novel, *If He Hollers Let Him Go*, demonstrates, is not so easily categorized. Even though Himes was undoubtedly influenced by Wright, he is not one of Wright's imitators. In fact, *If He Hollers Let Him Go* is written in reaction to *Native Son* and at many points is in direct contrast to it. Himes writes intensely about the fear and anger he has experienced but he is not so subjective that structure is sacrificed: *If He Hollers Let Him Go* is carried forward on a sequence of dreams that contributes both structural and thematic unity. And "Himes is . . . a

more deliberate prose stylist than Wright," the critic
Edward Margolies argues. "He seldom intrudes, mor-
alizes, or explains. His characters are usually sufficiently articulate to say what they mean—and what
they mean issues often enough from their character
and intelligence."[3] Instead of being grotesques,
Himes's characters often seem obsessed with a desire
to be ordinary (which, admittedly, may be grotesque-
ness of another sort), and they are always drawn in-
dividually enough, with sufficient potential control
over their environment, that the reader, black or white,
is never led to feel directly responsible. For Himes
the question of responsibility is not quite so simple,
nor are racial attitudes easily altered—as a reading of
If He Hollers Let Him Go reveals. But first it is helpful
to consider the book in another context.

One of the recurring complaints about the American novel since 1940 is that there has been a failure to
successfully objectify in fiction the harrowing global
events that have followed one upon another. A specific
complaint centers on the failure to produce a lasting
and powerful novel about World War II. Norman
Mailer's *The Naked and the Dead* is sometimes men-
tioned in response to this criticism along with (and
even more halfheartedly) Irwin Shaw's *The Young
Lions*. Himes's *If He Hollers Let Him Go* is not ordinarily considered in discussions of this sort because the
setting is Los Angeles, the hero is a shipyard worker,
and as close to military duty as Himes takes his protagonist is on the last page when a policeman is
marching Bob Jones and two Mexicans to an induction
center. But the war-effort atmosphere Himes evokes in
the California shipyards, the suspicion Bob Jones has,
when he sees American Japanese being interned in
concentration camps, that his people will be next, and
the ironic presence of the constant warfare within Bob

himself simply because he is a black man while he is
supposedly a loyal contributor to the external war
against worldwide fascism—all this makes Himes's
novel a vicious and bitter commentary on American
involvement in World War II.

Bob Jones, articulate, two years of college, a leaderman at Atlas Ship, and desperately wanting simply
to get along, to be left alone, is dreaming as the novel
opens. It is Monday morning. Bob sleeps on one side
and dreams of a black dog on a wire leash. He rolls
over onto the other side and dreams about being inter-
rogated for the killing of a white man in a war plant.
The killer is described as black, with a crippled leg.
Bob turns onto his back and dreams of asking two
white men for work. They laugh because he lacks the
tools for the job. Margolies is correct in emphasizing
that these dreams of tethered dogs, crippled men, and
rejection underscore Bob's main torment—"his intellectual awareness of what happens to him coupled
with his inability to act to save himself."⁴ But they also
point to a nightmarish vision of American society as an
enormous war factory within which a racial war far
more significant and intense than the one raging in the
Pacific or the one being practiced more quietly at
Auschwitz is going on. And a worker who wakes up
with fear every morning may snap his leash, may find
his tools, may pull the trigger, and may get away in a
new Buick instead of on a crippled leg. He may—but
as Bob Jones finds out as he wakes from his nightmares into an even greater one, he won't.

Why the fear? Why the anger? Bob has a good
job. He has had two years of college. He has a draft
deferment because, as a defense worker, he is impor
tant to national security. And he is in Los Angeles, not
Little Rock. It is Los Angeles for one thing. He left
Cleveland thinking L.A. would be different, a place

where he could put his racial self-consciousness out of his mind. But he found that, if anything, the rejection, because it was more subtle was worse. What compounded it was hearing Japanese children sing "God Bless America" one day and seeing them being sent along with their parents to internment compounds the next. He realized he was nearly the same color as the Japanese-Americans. After that he studied the faces of white Americans on the streets more closely. What he saw is "that crazy, wild-eyed unleashed hatred that the first Jap bomb on Pearl Harbor let loose in a flood. All that tight, crazy feeling of race as thick in the street as gas fumes. Every time I stepped outside I saw a challenge I had to accept or ignore. Every day I had to make one decision a thousand times: *Is it now? Is now the time?*"[5] All he wants is to be ignored by white America; but he fears that he will not be, that he is part of a war machine that is fueled by racial hatred as much as it is by love of freedom or a commitment to the preservation of democracy.

He is late for work. He backs his '42 Buick Roadmaster out of the garage and races to pick up his riders, all black and all members of his work crew. The battlefield atmosphere builds. "Is you ready to face the enemy, that's what I wanna know?" one of his riders asks. "Is you ready to meet the man, that's what I mean."[6] The drive to work becomes a scramble for survival as Bob fights a battle of nerves against white drivers for position and advantage. He deliberately aims his car at white pedestrians. And all the while he is fighting a battle against time, a battle he loses; he pulls into the shipyard parking lot at five after eight.

He and his crew are installing ventilation equipment in the shower compartments deep within a floating drydock. The working conditions are intense and violent with minimal clearance between decks, weld-

ing lines running everywhere, blowers, chippers, and
burners all working at once, and a maze of passage-
ways cluttered with unfinished and unattached metal
parts. As if this is not hell enough for Bob, he has to
cope with a supervisor, Kelly, who had tried to block
his promotion to leaderman, and with white workers
who will not step aside for him to pass.

Bob's problems begin right away that Monday
morning. One of his men needs a tacker to help him,
but Bob knows that none of the tacker leaders will
assign a white tacker to an all-black work gang. Bob
patiently keeps asking until he is allowed to recruit a
white woman worker named Madge. When he tells
her of her assignment, she says she will not work for a
nigger. Bob loses his temper, calls her a cracker bitch,
and winds up in the department superintendent's
office for cursing a woman on the job. MacDougal, the
superintendent, tells him that he is not doing what he
was promoted to do—keep down the trouble between
white and black workers—and that he will be demoted to mechanic starting the next week. Not only
that, Bob will lose his job deferment and become eligible for the draft.

The lunch whistle blows as Bob leaves the office,
and he decides to look for a crap game to take his
mind off his trouble. He gets into a dispute over
cocked dice and gets knocked out by Johnny Stoddart,
a tall blond man from the copper shop. When Bob
comes to, he borrows a knife and heads for the copper
shop. He faces Stoddart but backs off, deciding that it
would be better to kill him later when he knew Stoddart had no chance and could expect no mercy. "I
wanted him to feel as scared and powerless and un-
protected as I felt every goddamned morning I woke
up," Bob remembers. "I wanted him to know how it
felt to die without a chance, how it felt to look death

in the face and know it was coming and know there wasn't anything he could do but sit there and take it like I had to take it from Kelly and Hank and Mac and the cracker bitch because nobody was going to help him or stop it or do anything about it at all."[7] This decision is like a declaration of war, and Bob experiences a rush of freedom.

He punches out of the shipyard and gets into his car. The drive away from the plant is in pleasant contrast to the drive in. The nature of the battle has changed, and Bob has a sense of well-being and control. He stops for a big steak and some drinks, then he goes back to his room, changes his clothes, and picks up his .38 Special. He goes out and strolls along Central Avenue watching the weedheads, the hustlers, the pimps, and the gamblers. At 4:30 he is back in his car outside the parking lot at Atlas, waiting for his man. Bob sees Stoddart get into a gray Ford and follows the car to a house in Huntington Park, where Stoddart gets out, takes two steps, turns and sees Bob, who slowly emerges from the Buick with his pistol. The white man heads for his front steps where he is met by his wife and children, ducks inside, and bolts the door. Bob once again decides to let him wait. He tells two old ladies who are walking past on the sidewalk that it is a nice day. And he tells himself that as long as the private war he has declared continues, as long as he knows that someday he will kill Stoddart, nothing will bother him.

He calls up one of the best hotels in town and makes reservations for two that night. He next calls his girl, Alice, and tells her to dress for a special evening. Alice, who can pass for white, lives with her father, a successful black physician, and her mother, a woman who honestly believes that whites are helping blacks earn their equality and that Bob should take advantage of the many opportunities he has been offered. He resists getting into an argument with her, because he knows she would not understand his new battle plan.

Alice is no more willing to understand it when she and Bob pull up to the front door of the hotel. She is shocked at what he intends to do and is afraid to go in, but Bob gives her no choice. The meal is a battle of nerves for Bob and Alice, and when the check comes, a piece of paper is clipped to it telling Bob that he has received service this time but that the hotel does not want him as a customer in the future.

Alice is disgusted with Bob and takes the wheel on the drive back, speeding to show her anger. They are stopped by a patrol car, addressed as coons by the officer, hauled to the police station, and forced to put up cash bail. Alice then takes him to meet some friends of hers at a cottage on San Pedro. Bob, to his disgust, finds out that the friends—two girls and Chuck, a slim young man—are homosexuals, and that Alice is more than comfortable in their presence. He slaps Alice, hits Chuck, and leaves. Bob's Monday is complete—he is demoted from his job as leaderman, has pledged himself to a murder pact, has eaten dinner in a jim crow hotel, and has learned, he thinks, that the girl he plans to marry is a lesbian.

These turns in the life of Bob Jones are sudden and almost seem like too much for a single day. Joseph Warren Beach in his review of the novel objected to the "melodramatic cliches"[8] that appear again and again; but what seems like melodrama is simply Himes's way of emphasizing that for a character like Bob, who is engaged in a constant battle with himself and with a culture that seems determined to keep him in his place, life is one damned and abrupt thing after another because he lives in a combat zone.

That night Bob dreams again, this time of being beaten by two white southerners who are supervised by the shipyard president dressed up as an army general. Two old colored couples come walking past and stop to agree with the general that some boys like Bob do get into trouble, but good folks like them are not causing any problems. Bob is thrown into a squad car and, when it is started, he wakes up. This dream, like all of the dreams in the novel, underscores the resemblance between the nightmares Bob suffers through each night and the nightmare world he wakes up to each day. He sleeps like a shell-shocked soldier and wakes up each morning not quite certain about where he is and which is real—the dream or the morning light.

Alice calls and tells Bob she is sorry, but Bob insults her and she hangs up. He decides not to report for work and goes instead to the Rust Room, a bar in Little Tokyo, where he witnesses one of those complicated racially charged scenes that occur again and again in Himes's novels. A young white girl, blond, looking like a runaway, comes into the bar with two soldiers. She gets high on two beers and starts eying all the black men in the place. When she gets up to play the jukebox and stands there shaking herself to the music, a black man is suddenly at her side and insists on paying for the music himself. She smiles at him, and every pimp and hustler in the bar is watching her. One of the soldiers makes her sit down, but soon she is back at the jukebox and this time she has two black men pushing the buttons for her. The soldiers see what is happening and try to leave without her. The manager stops them and says that they will have to take her with them. She does not want to go. One of the soldiers refers to the bar as a nigger joint and fists tighten on bottles and glasses up and down

the bar. The manager knows that if a fight breaks out
he will lose his liquor license; not only that, if the
manager hits one of the soldiers and hurts him, if there
is any kind of incident in which the white girl is injured, the result would be a riot. White GIs would
overrun the district as they did in the zoot suit riots
that had recently swept the Mexican barrios. And all
this because of a white girl, black men, and the erotic
taboo—now ancient in American culture—that is more
basic to racial guilt and oppression than most Americans, black or white, will admit. But Bob Jones sees it
and he knows it, not only because his girl friend can
pass for white and he is given the evil eye almost
everywhere he goes with her, but because a white
woman no better than the little blond in the bar
caused his demotion the day before. The bitter memory of Madge hits him. "The indignity of it, the gut-
ting of my pride, what a nigger had to take just to
keep on living in the goddamned world," he reflected.
"I thought about killing the white boy again, but it
didn't do anything at all for me now. It seemed child-
ish, ridiculous, so completely futile; I couldn't kill all
the white folks, that was a cinch."[9] He sits there, the
scared feeling coming back to remind him he is a
black man, trapped by his own weakness.

He decides to go see Alice. Three of her friends,
who, like Alice, are social workers, are at her house. As
if to counterpoint the scene Bob has just witnessed,
they ask him what he thinks should be done to allevi-
ate the conditions in Little Tokyo. Better health care?
Public housing? Recreation programs? Bob sits there
and looks at them as if he cannot believe it. He tells
them that if he knew any solution for the race problem, he would sure enough use it for himself. Through
this scene and the preceding one Himes effectively
answers the critics who attacked him for not proposing

solutions to the problems he so bitterly raises. The very way he presents the problem—through the incident in the Rust Room, for example—explains the difficulty in finding the solution. Bob's own problems are further complicated when another social worker shows up, Tom Leighton, a white man with whom, Bob suspects, Alice is having an affair.

Leighton tries to get Bob talking about racial tension and Bob tells him that the only way out seems to be for blacks to make whites respect them and that the only way to do that is through force. Leighton wants to argue and Bob responds with a gesture that makes Alice's co-workers, including Leighton, get up and leave. Alice tells Bob that he is a "filthy Negro"[10] and that he should repress his anger in favor of his future and go back to college. She talks to him like a caseworker, but then she softens and tells him that she loves him, that she is not a lesbian, and that she does not want to lose him. He tells her about Madge and how he has lost the leaderman's job and tries to explain why he has been acting the way he has. But Alice, who has accepted the integrationist line of the 1940s (that blacks have to patiently earn equality), asks him to apologize to the girl. After all, Alice's father knows the president of the company. If Bob humbles himself, perhaps he will eventually be reinstated as leaderman, and, anyway, apology is the only choice Alice will give him if he wants them to stay together.

That night Bob dreams again. Alice shrinks before his eyes into a tiny form, almost a rag doll. When he looks up, millions of white women are staring at him. He wakes up thinking of Madge. He picks up his riders and goes to work, where he tries his last reasonable approach. He asks the union steward to tell Madge she has to work with blacks. The steward, a Jew who talks leftist rhetoric but refuses to admit he is a communist, says he will talk to her but not in Bob's presence. Bob tells him to go to hell and gets Madge's home address from another worker—a white man who looks at him knowingly. Bob decides he is going to punish her, that he's "going to have to make her as low as a white whore in a Negro slum—a scrummy two-dollar whore. . . . so I could keep looking the white folks in the face."[11] He goes over to where she is working, but he loses his nerve when he confronts her with her "eyes as wide as Oklahoma." He is unable to speak, unable to set up the date. "She was pure white Texas," he explained, "And I was black. And a white man was standing there. I never knew before how good a job the white folks had done on me."[12] To have her, to get even, he must challenge her color, and at that moment he cannot do it.

Unmanned, frustrated, Bob picks up a club and goes after Johnny Stoddart, the man in the copper shop. Stoddart is out. Bob leaves the shop, flings the club down, and accidentally almost hits Stoddart who is on his way back. The look of fear on Stoddart's face is satisfaction enough for Bob, and he walks away. At least one white man in the world is living with the kind of fear Bob lives with every day.

That evening he stops for a drink in a bar, plays King Cole's "I'm Lost" on the jukebox, and knows that he is fueling up to go after Madge.

He climbs the stairs to her room in a seedy hotel and knocks on her door. He demands to be let in and pushes Madge down on the bed. Her hair is in curlers, she is wearing a scruffy robe, and she looks much older than she does at work. She struggles free and pulls off her robe. As he stares at her sagging body, she says, "This'll get you lynched in Texas."[13] She urges him to rape her, but the very word scares him. Lynching,

Texas, rape—it is more than the nervous system of an educated black man like Bob, who knows about the Scottsboro boys, and has gotten in on discussions of *Native Son*, can tolerate. The culture he has grown up in has done a good job on him; he runs from the room and out to his car. In a scene that is indeed a grim parody of Bigger Thomas's predicament in *Native Son* and also an extended parody of all the black man-white woman scenarios that lurk in the American subconscious, Madge runs after him and tries to get into his car. Bob hits the gas, and he does not look back.

He dreams that night of a young white and a young black fighting. The black has a long knife and the white youth seems to have nothing. Then the white is chasing the black and hitting him again and again with a downward stroke of his fist. But Bob sees that the white is grasping a penknife with a quarter-inch blade, and he is inflicting dozens of tiny stab wounds. Himes once again uses the dream in a realistic way to emphasize the hopeless feeling with which Bob wakes up. Bob's hangover gives him the honesty of a man facing death and he tries to think clearly about the battle he has been caught up in. He knows that unless he overcomes his hatred for whites that there is no place for him. He thinks of people like Alice and her parents who have, in a sense, overcome their color by adjusting themselves to the limitations white society has placed on them. Not a hard thing to do, reasons Bob—it is just a matter of accepting one's fate as a black man. And fate is something over which the individual has no control. Worship the black heritage, accept segregation, and wait for the whites to appreciate the effort enough to open the door all the way. But Bob has not learned things that way. He has learned about the United States the same as whites have, and he has thought along with them that George

Washington is the father of *his* country. He read the
Hearst papers and believed what they said about the
need to fight the Nazis in Europe. He had even believed Westbrook Pegler. "That was the hell of it," Bob
thought, "the white folks had drummed more into me
than they'd been able to scare out."[14] But it is as if
whites did not expect blacks, despite the education
both races shared, to have these ideas. Bob knew they
thought of him in terms of Africa, but not in terms of
the United States, even though Bob had forgotten his
African origins as much as they had forgotten their
European ones. Alice's logic was apparent to him, but
accommodation still seemed like betrayal, like collaboration—the kind of collaboration that was going
on in France with the Nazis.

Bob knows he could marry Alice, finish college, go
to law school and become "a successful colored man."
But he also knows that one day it would not be
enough, because he still would not be able to walk
down certain streets and live in certain houses. He
would not be able to politely proposition Lana Turner
without having a billy club broken over his head.
"Anyone who wanted to could be nigger-rich, nigger-
important, have their Jim Crow religion, and go to
nigger heaven,"[15] he concluded. What he wants, and
all he wants, is to be an ordinary man distinguished
neither by color nor ambition and able to go places
without being noticed. It is, as Bob knows, a foolish
notion.

He is jumpy when he gets to work, and confused.
He finds Tebbel, the white leaderman who is his re-
placement, cursing out the Jews. Bob has a headache
and stumbles about over broken pieces of pipe, weld-
ing torches flashing all around. He thinks of quitting.
He goes looking for Madge, tries to think of Alice and
Leighton. At a quarter to twelve he is told that there is

a call for him. It is Alice and she agrees to meet him at
a drive-in for lunch. He is happy to see her and for the
first time that day, the first time all week he thinks
that things might turn out all right. But again he notices the white people in the surrounding cars staring
at them. Alice tells him that he is maladjusted, that he
must learn to accept actual conditions. Bob feels like a
machine being run by whites; they push all the buttons and he responds every time. Alice explains that he
must be content with the control he can exert within
his own pattern. The argument is too tedious, too
much to get into, and Bob has gone through too much
since Monday. He asks her to marry him as soon as
possible; he believes that if she is his wife he can face
what he has to face, that he can go back to work at
peace with himself. He sees himself as a lawyer pleading for a black youth; when he gets there and is standing in front of the jury, things will have changed.

Bob goes back to Atlas, talks to MacDougal in the
superintendent's office, and tells him that he is getting
married and that he wants to stay on the job. Mac-
Dougal knows he has Bob where he wants him and
tells him that yes, if he cooperates, he might eventually get his leaderman's job back. Bob does not like
what he hears, but he listens. He finds his crew and
discovers that they are working far harder than they
ever did for him because Tebbel has gotten them a
better job. It is apparent to Bob that Kelly is trying to
sell the black workers on Tebbel so that they will not
want Bob back. But Bob has to accept what is happening. He starts for the superstructure to look the new
job over.

As Bob is walking past a closed door, he notices
an extension cord going underneath it. He looks inside
and there is Madge sleeping on a bunk. She sees him
and tells him to shut the door behind him. He tries to

get out, but she stops him just as he hears footsteps coming down the corridor. She locks the door. A Navy inspector stops outside, sees the cord, tries the handle, and insists that the door be opened. Madge knocks Bob down and starts screaming rape. The inspector has a welder burn the door open as Madge engages Bob in a fake struggle. Bob breaks out, but he is hit on the head with a ballpeen hammer.

He comes to in the company infirmary with a guard watching him. Somehow he manages to escape from the gatekeepers who are holding him for the police. He needs no excuse for his desperation: "A white woman yelling, 'Rape,' and a Negro caught locked in the room. The whole structure of American thought was against me; American tradition had convicted me a hundred years before."[16] He runs to his car and evades pursuit. He calls home, but Ella Mae, from whom Bob is renting his room, tells him not to show up—the police are there. He calls Alice and tells her what happened. She doubts his innocence and tells him she will not help him run away, and, besides, if he is innocent, she has enough confidence in American justice to believe that he will be acquitted. She will not give him any escape money, but she will try to get him a good lawyer. He hangs up and drives into the ghetto. Then he decides he will go out and kill Stoddart to at least give them something to hang him for. But as he stops at a red light in a white neighborhood, a police cruiser pulls alongside. As soon as the officers see that he is black, they pull him over. They find the pistol and take him in.

That night in his cell he dreams of shooting Stoddart. He is caught by a laughing Marine sergeant who asks him what he did. Bob tells him he killed a white man because he called him nigger, and that he has also raped a white woman. "Hell I've raped all kinda women," the laughing sergeant says, "white women, black women, yellow women, red women, and the only reason I ain't raped no green women is 'cause I couldn't find none. I done killed all kinda sonabitches raped all kinda women."[17] And then he points to his chest where he wears the Purple Heart, the Bronze Star, the Presidential Memorial Citation, and a Good Conduct medal. But one thing he has not done—killed a nigger, which he is about to do as Bob wakes up on the floor. With this dream, Himes brings the irony in the kind of war the sergeant has been fighting and in Bob's more private war to its highest point. Bob is about to be lynched for war crimes of one sort that he did not even commit; the sergeant is given medals for crimes of a worse sort that he joyfully confesses to.

Bob is told that the judge is to see him right away. There Bob learns that the president of the corporation has interceded. The president tells the judge that he has talked with Madge and that she has decided not to press charges because it would cause increased racial tension at the plant—just the thing that is not needed because it would interfere with the war effort. The judge turns to Bob and lectures him on how he has betrayed the trust that was placed in him as the first black leaderman at Atlas and how he has consequently delayed the rapid progress of his people. But the judge will give him a break—Bob will be allowed to enlist in the army on the condition that he promises to stay away from white women. And Bob, along with the two Mexicans who are waiting at the police desk, is on his way to become a soldier and get his chance at the real war. One Mexican asks him how he is doing. "I'm still here," Bob says.[18]

The ending of the novel is a reiteration of the nightmare sequence that structures the book. Bob's story encompasses five days and each day is preceded by a dream or a set of dreams. He cannot sleep without having the agony of his waking hours imaged in grotesque scenarios inspired by the fear and despair that he must deal with in just getting out of bed and starting to think about all those white faces in the cars on the expressway, the compacted work space he and his crew are assigned to because it is "nigger work," the tight line he must walk as a leaderman in dealing with white superintendents and white women workers, and even the problem of acceptance he has with Alice, who wants him to be as much like her as is possible— that is, almost white. These dreams begin and end his work days, and as bizarre as some of them are, they merge increasingly with his conscious experience, and by the end of the novel, the reader recalls Bob's story as one extended nightmare. And it is with the dazed and unbelieving voice of the sleeper who wakes from scenes of terror to find that he is still there even though cold sweat is running from him that Bob speaks when it is all over.

But will he dream again? Is Bob's nightmare over? *If He Hollers Let Him Go* is a war novel, and when the novel ends, the war is still being fought, both Bob's war and the war to which he is being sent. The test of courage Bob has endured is not unlike that of Henry Fleming in *The Red Badge of Courage*. But despite the fear that dogs him all the way, Bob has not actually turned from the fight, although he is offered little chance to be heroic. The enemy will not fight fairly and Bob can never quite find a battle line to get behind. Besides, as a soldier in the racial war, Bob has been brainwashed by the opposition. He can make Stoddart afraid, but he cannot pull the trigger except in fantasy. Just as he cannot kill a white man, he cannot rape a white woman. What is ironic is that he winds up in jail as a suspected or potential killer (the police find the revolver in the glove compartment of his car) and as an accused rapist (when, in a sense, he is a rape victim). So Bob is defeated at every step, and at the end he has won nothing—nor is it likely that he ever will. His dreams are confused, his life is confused, and, on the final page of his story, he is simply being marched off, the law at his back.

But Bob is still there, as he himself attests so significantly, and he represents an aspect of black consciousness that sooner or later must be dealt with. But Himes is not at all certain in the novel that the Bob Joneses will be dealt with fairly. The internment camp figures prominently in Bob's thoughts and it is apparent that the kind of accommodation for which Alice and her parents have such hope is never going to amount to much. Bob Jones is not like Wright's Bigger Thomas; he is not illiterate and he does not quite seem such a victim of his environment. Bob, after all, could follow Alice's lines; he could make choices that would enable him to live quite comfortably. Law school is easily enough within his reach. Unlike Bigger, he is not confused by ideas, and Bob's speech is much more cultured than that of the whites with whom he works. But just as much as Bigger, he is brought down by circumstances. Bigger pushes open the door of Mary Dalton's room and is trapped in compromising circumstances with a white woman. Bob does the same when he gets curious about the extension cord underneath the door of the room in which he finds Madge sleeping. Both of them—the young tough from the rat-infested slums of Chicago's South Side and the college-educated leaderman—panic, flee, and are apprehended. Bigger is executed and Bob is allowed to live on, not quite so much the victim, his plight not so clearly apparent, but still a threat to the Stoddarts and the Madges and to himself.

But as far as society is concerned, the threat is an exaggerated one. Bob comes on at times like a bomb about to go off, but he is a dud; he has been defused. For all of his violent impulses, for all of his hatred of the system that represses him at almost every turn, he does not have it in him to be a rapist, a killer, or a revolutionist. He is ordinary. His very name—Bob Jones—suggests his ordinariness. And his ambition is simply to be a common Joe. If he could just be accepted as no one unusual, he would be content to spend the rest of his life working in the shipyard and going home to Alice and the kids. He has been educated to believe in America, to believe in freedom, money, a new car. He wants nothing to do with communism and even makes fun of the union steward's watered-down Marxism. But because he is black, and simply because of that, these ideas and attitudes seem a little absurd. He cannot be treated as an ordinary person in the sense that he defines the term. And because he is denied this dream and all dreams except nightmares, it is understandable that he will turn violent, that he will grab a pistol and go after the next white man who calls him nigger. But Bob has received another kind of education, one he hardly knows about, one he in fact discovers in the course of the novel. He has been taught what it means for a black man to kill a white man. He has learned the meaning of rape so well that he runs from a worn-out Texas blonde without even having to tell his feet to move. And here is the split in Bob's personality; he has learned patterns of belief and desire that effectively cancel each other out to—and the words are surprisingly apt—keep him in his place. White America do not fear; black America do not look for your hero here.

One reviewer of *If He Hollers Let Him Go* wrote that "It is Bob Jones's inability to keep on an even keel that alienates a good deal of the reader's sympathy for him."[19] But it is this very inability that makes Bob memorable, makes him seem more an individual than a type, even though one of Himes's intentions is to make the war-time scenes through which Bob passes representative of conditions that a black man, given Bob's responsibility at Atlas Ship, would have to face. Bob is a manic-depressive, a compulsive drinker, and, among other things, a maniacal driver. There is little about him that is amusing and the only jokes he seems to hear are racial. He reacts with disgust both to the ghetto world of Central Avenue and the suburban world of Alice's parents. And his sudden fits of ineffectual rage have a hint of childishness about them. But these defects go a long way toward humanizing Bob and making him believable. He is not a symbolic figure caught in a revolutionary battle plan; he is fighting, despite its obvious universality, a one-man war, and because of this there can be for him no such thing as an even keel. He will, in all likelihood, destroy himself before he destroys anyone else, and this is the real danger, the real tragedy as far as Bob is concerned. And this is one of the most pervasive criticisms Himes makes of American society, that the black man in his anger unknowingly turns on himself, that his life is wired for destruction.

If He Hollers Let Him Go is a social protest novel somewhat in the tradition of the proletarian, toughguy novels of the 1930s. It inevitably falls into this category with its depiction of the shipyard, the ghetto, and the sprawl of Los Angeles. Bob, as much as many of the characters in novels by James M. Cain, Jack Conroy, or Michael Gold, reacts to an unreceptive world in a violent way and uses language that is unremittingly tough in describing the conditions of that world. When Bob is waking up that first day, for example, he hears Ella Mae feeding her baby and tells us, "All I could hear was the sound of the baby sucking greedily, and I thought if they really wanted to give him a break they'd cut his throat and bury him in the back yard before he got old enough to know he was a nigger."[20] Such a reaction and such language contribute to the harsh mood of protest that is present in most of Himes's writing and makes his bitterness seem all the more extreme and understandable. But *If He Hollers Let Him Go* differs from much social-protest literature in that it is documentary without being propagandistic. Himes presents conditions, makes Bob's problems apparent enough, but offers no solution other than the sheer survival capabilities Bob demonstrates. In his next novel, *Lonely Crusade*, Himes tried to explain why his first book does not go very far beyond sheer exposition in its treatment of Bob's predicament.

Lonely Crusade seems at first like a continuation of *If He Hollers Let Him Go*. The setting is Los Angeles in the spring of 1943, the impact of the war on the consciousness of the main characters is considerable, the war effort is a constant factor in the plot, and the hero, Lee Gordon, a black union organizer, is an expression of the same personality type as Bob. Lee is educated, racially obsessed, troubled by a nagging sense of inferiority, and given to vicious expressions of outrage. But Lee's story differs considerably from Bob's in that it deals more extensively with ideas (Marxism and existentialism) and social movements (unionism). More important, *Lonely Crusade* offers a solution to the overwhelming theme of hopelessness that runs through Bob's life, and it presents this solution through a series of philosophical dialogues and representative actions that result in an often horrifying but ultimately insightful vivisection of the black man's

obsession with his history of oppression and his hope
for the future.

It was the Communist Party that seemed to offer
hope to many blacks in the 1930s and 1940s, and it is
Himes's reaction to communist activities and programs
that provides Lee Gordon with conflict after conflict.
During the 1930s, Himes could hardly avoid being
drawn toward the Communist Party, which aggres-
sively tried to recruit writers and Negroes. Several
front organizations such as the American Writers'
Congress, the League of American Writers, and the
John Reed Clubs as well as such journals as *New
Masses* existed in part to attract Himes's generation.
The party's activities on behalf of blacks in general
included the League of Struggle for Negro Rights and
its active defense of the Scottsboro boys. In addition,
it took over the National Negro Congress and also ran
a black vice-presidential candidate in the national
elections of 1932 and 1936. Many blacks joined the
party, Richard Wright one of them (becoming a member in 1934). Wright believed that the party "provided
him with an intellectual framework for understanding
his life as a Negro."[21]

In addition to identifying the black man with the
oppressed classes out of which revolution usually
springs, the Communist Party in its opposition to fascism during the 1930s (more pointedly, its opposition
to Hitler) was attractive to blacks because of its opposition to the fascist theories of white supremacy. In
addition, the party appealed to black nationalist sen-
timents among American Negroes through its position
that the "Negro problem" in the United States must be
viewed as part of the larger problem of imperialism.
Negroes in the United States, it was argued, are the
victims of a colonial power; they are in effect a nation
within a nation, and are in need of liberation. The

party consequently advocated the establishment of a
Negro Soviet Republic somewhere in the American
South. "As a metaphor, or as a myth, the idea of a
separate Negro nation expresses a separatist impulse
deeply embedded in Negro psychology," Bone writes,[22]
and many black intellectuals (again including
Wright) embraced the separatist solution offered by
the Communist Party. But perhaps the basic appeal of
the party was not the extremism of separatism, but
simply the appeal of unity, a remedy for the destructive sense of loneliness that almost every black writer
of the time attested to. In "I tried to Be a Communist,"
Wright explained that one reason why he joined the
party was that it "did not say 'Be like us and we will
like you, maybe.' It said: 'If you possess enough courage to speak out what you are, you will find that you
are not alone.' "[23]

To a certain extent, *Native Son* resulted from the
kind of courage Wright derived from his involvement
in the party. And many of the novels by black writers
that followed *Native Son* and spoke out in much the
same way can be partially attributed to the influence
that the party had on black artists. Wilson Record in
The Negro and the Communist Party explains the influence in terms of the party line: "It was with the
struggle of this Negro nation to achieve its manhood
that the Negro artists and intellectuals were to be concerned. Its trials, its tribulations, its sufferings,—these
were to be the major themes of novels, of music, of
other creative forms. To select other themes was tan-
tamount to the betrayal of the race."[24]

But by the end of the 1930s and most certainly by
the early 1940s many blacks became disillusioned with
the communist program mainly because of several
awkward policy shifts. The party stand against fascism
and white supremacy was seriously compromised by

the signing of the Russo-German nonaggression pact in 1939. And then, when Hitler subsequently invaded the Soviet Union, the party suspended its support of civil rights in favor of national unity, promising that once the war was over, the old program would go back into effect. This softening of the party line on racism made many blacks suspicious of what appeared to be outright betrayal. Wright, Ellison, Himes, and many others drifted away from the party, and some, like Himes, became openly scornful of what the party had done to many of the blacks who had supported it so faithfully and so hopefully. One of the greatest fears Lee Gordon has in *Lonely Crusade* is that he will be used by the party for purposes that have nothing to do with the liberation of himself or his race. He suspects that the party has its own ends, most of which are dictated by the Russian ruling class, and that it is willing to manipulate Marxism in such a way that those ends most likely will not be his own or those of his people.

Himes develops his opinions on communism through a novel that is reminiscent of the "strike" novels of the 1930s in its treatment of the problems of union organization, the opposition of the bosses, and the brutality of the police. In tone, development of minor characters, and structure, *Lonely Crusade* resembles Mary Horton Vorse's *Strike* (1930), William Rollins's *The Shadow Before* (1934), Robert Cantwell's *The Land of Plenty* (1934), Meyer Levin's *Citizens* (1940), and, perhaps the best novel of this type, John Steinbeck's *In Dubious Battle* (1936). As Walter Rideout points out in *The Radical Novel in the United States, 1900–1954*, the trajectory of the strike novel is "aptly designed for artistic expression. The storm gathers, the initial clash occurs, the struggle veers back and forth, producing suspense as the advantage goes now to this side, now to that; the climax is reached when the strike succeeds or is broken, and the action thereafter drops swiftly."[25] Although *Lonely Crusade* centers on a union organizing drive instead of a strike, the movement toward the demonstration rally that is scheduled for the morning of the election day is essentially the same as the relentless development of tension in the strike novels.

In another sense, however, *Lonely Crusade* is not a typical proletarian novel. For one thing, Lee Gordon is an educated man who does not want to be identified with the workers, black or white, and is actually embarrassed by the crudity of the very people he is trying to organize. At the start of the novel he is much more involved in his own problems as a black man than he is in the plight of the workers at Comstock Aircraft. For another thing, *Lonely Crusade* is a philosophical novel that takes the reader through a series of dialogues involving Lee and various characters, who contribute to Lee's growing awareness not of the problems between management and labor but to his awareness of the problem of himself and the definition of his own reality. The Negro problem, unionization, and communism are all eventually subordinated to the existential commitment with which the novel concludes. But for Lee Gordon, the movement toward that conclusion represents an agonizing step-by-step progression toward an understanding of his own personality, that of his race, and ultimately that of all men.

Lee has been hired as a union organizer, a job that represents not only his first chance at important work but also vindication of the effort he had made in obtaining his college degree; at last he had a job that matched up to his qualifications. But there is one complication: it is a "Negro First" job—that is, Lee is

the first black to be hired as a full-time organizer by
the union. His initial elation at being hired diminishes
when he realizes the harassment he will have to face in
the predominantly white world of union structure and
management. But he hopes his ability to handle the
job will enable him to gain the respect of his wife,
Ruth, whom he has never quite been able to support
and who has been supporting him by working as a
women's counselor in a Los Angeles factory. Lee suffers from the classic sense of inferiority and guilt
forced upon the black male by a white society that has
denied him the economic opportunity to be a "man" to
his wife. The consequence has been a brutalization of
the relationship between Lee and Ruth. Out of frustration, he has repeatedly beaten her. The night before
his first day as an organizer, he tries to take the edge
off his anxiety by making love to her; but she is indif-
ferent. To Ruth, her husband's desire, which seemed
to be greatest when he felt most racially frustrated,
only makes her feel defeated and whorish. Like Bob in
If He Hollers Let Him Go, Lee lives in constant tension, angry at society for what it has done to him and
angry at himself for taking it, his hatred running two
ways.

He wakes up to anger and mistake. Smitty, the
union council secretary, is outside, honking for him.
Lee curses himself; he has forgotten to set his alarm
and he knows what Smitty must be thinking about
blacks always being late. The rain outside matches
Lee's mood as he and Smitty drive toward the Comstock plant, but on the way he engages in the first of
the dialogues that constitute his education. Lee is
caught up in brooding over his own problems, scarcely
listening to what Smitty has to say and almost laughing when Smitty tells him, "Lee, you might say the
working class of the world depends on us here. As

Comstock goes, the West Coast goes. As the West Coast goes, the nation goes. As the nation goes, the world goes."[26] Lee does not see where he fits in; to him organizing is a job, not a matter of moral commitment. Because of his racial consciousness, he does not believe he can act for all men, perhaps not even for his own people, perhaps only for himself. Lee's attitudes have no place in Smitty's concept of unionization.

The word *union* appears on almost every page of the novel and it comes to take on a significance beyond its basic connotations of labor organization. At the start of the book, Lee is himself disorganized. He has no sense of unity. He and his wife are at odds, he is resentful of the way he has been forced to live by white society in the United States, and he is torn within by self-hatred and feelings of inadequacy. As his story progresses and he is drawn into union activities of the sort Smitty stands for, Lee moves toward unity on all levels. He and Ruth become closer in their understanding of one another, he begins to believe in the possibility of friendship and trust between whites and blacks, and he becomes more unified in personality. But this movement is a painful one, and Lee approaches disunity and dissolution on all three levels.

At the one-room shack outside the Comstock gates that serves as headquarters for the local, Lee meets another man who is to engage him in the second dialogue of the novel—Joe Ptak, a toughened ex-steel mill worker assigned by the National to help in the Comstock drive. After recording the names and addresses of workers off the graveyard shift who stop by the shack to join up, Joe and Lee go out to a nearby bar and grill to talk. Joe defines the issues for Lee, and it is here that Lee learns what he is up against. Most of the workers are from the south and they believe what

they read in the papers—that unionization is associated with communism. They are making more money
than ever before and the company, to head off unionization, has adopted a fair system of seniority and gives
insurance and accident benefits. At the time, conditions are good, but the workers do not realize that the
company executives, especially Foster, a retired mil-
lionaire who is executive vice president in charge of
production, offer good wages but no security. When
the war ends and labor is not such a premium, what
then? To avoid charges of discrimination, Foster has
hired three thousand black workers—an even ten percent of the force. But it is only ten percent, no more,
and almost all are working in the lowest grades. It is
Lee's job to organize the black workers, but he must
realize that the union has to be careful—it cannot ir-
ritate the southern whites who constitute the majority
of the plant employees. Lee must also be careful about
the communists. Joe warns that the party will probably assign another black man or a white woman to
work on Lee. And Foster may come at him another
way; Lee should not be surprised if Foster offers him a
better-paying job in order to buy him off and discredit
the union. "It's the future of the world," Joe tells him.
"All those boys dying and these rotten fascist bastards. . . . To hell with it! Our work is to get it done, not
to talk about it."[27]

That afternoon Lee distributes leaflets at the No. 2
gate. He felt little love for any people, black or white,
and the struggle of humanity seemed alien to him. He
was willing to let everyone go to hell; to him it is the
American way. But back at the shack, he finds out that
others do not share that opinion, at least as far as
letting Lee Gordon alone is concerned. A tall black
man with a scarred face insists on giving him a ride
home in an expensive coupe. His name is Luther Mc-

Gregor and he tells Lee that he has been assigned to work along with him. Lee is suspicious; he realizes at once that Luther is a communist, that he is the one Joe warned him about.

Lee's suspicions about communists and his pessimism about his own future—whether that outlined for him by the party or by his own ambition—had been with him for a long time. He had started grade school in Pasadena, the only black in his class. By the fourth grade he understood what his teachers were saying about him: that most black people in the world are cannibals and heathens. At fourteen he was caught hiding in the girls' locker room; he wanted to find out what was so different about white girls that he was never supposed to even think about looking at them. He was expelled from school and his parents were forced to leave the city. "He came to feel that the guilt or innocence of anything he might do would be subject wholly to the whim of white people," Himes writes. "It stained his whole existence with a sense of sudden disaster hanging just above his head, and never afterwards could he feel at ease in the company of white people."[28] His family moved to Los Angeles, and the summer after Lee's graduation from high school, his father, who was working as a janitor in a department store, was shot to death by a policeman who mistook him for a burglar. The family received a $1500 donation from sympathetic people, and Lee realized how little his father's life was worth.

Lee struggled through University of California at Los Angeles majoring in sociology; but when he graduated, the only jobs open were in domestic service, which he pridefully refused to enter. But when he married Ruth, he was forced to work at anything he could get—bus boy, porter, laborer in a spinach-canning factory, and finally a civil-service job in the post office. He joined the postal workers' union and was recruited by the communists, who argued that the party was against injustice, intolerance, and prejudice —an argument that was suspended in favor of an all-out effort to defeat Hitler when Germany attacked Russia. After that, the white southerners in the post office were harder than ever on the blacks who worked there. When he complained to the party officials, Lee found out that the antidiscrimination committee had been disbanded. Like Bob in *If He Hollers Let Him Go*, he notices white suspicion and hatred of all dark-skinned people increase after the Japanese attack on Pearl Harbor. When he is fired for muttering "Hitler" at a harassing postal superintendent, Lee asks the party for support and is refused. He is so angered and frustrated that the night Japanese planes are suppos-edly sighted near Santa Monica and the shore batteries open up, Lee shouts, "They're here! They're here! They're here! Oh, Goddammit, they're coming! Come on, you little bad bastards! Come on and take this city!"[26] Out of work, opposed to the war effort on racial grounds, Lee is humiliated when his wife gets her counseling job and he is simply another black man being supported by a long-suffering woman. But the union job might be a solution for him; and it turns out to be one—but not the way Lee expected.

The second day of the job, Luther gets permission from Joe to take Lee out visiting black workers at home. The union is willing to work along with the communists in recruiting new union members but not in promoting revolution. Lee comes to respect Luther's abilities in interviewing and persuading, especially his ability to confuse with a disconcerting question and then to answer with Marxist logic. But what impresses Lee most is his own ignorance of his race—how differ-ent each recruit is, how strangely some react to the very idea of an inter-racial union, and how suspicious many of them are of him. "And most of what he learned," Himes emphasizes, "was hurting knowledge. It brought fear and hurt and shame to learn of the beaten, ignorant Negro laborer, so indoctrinated with the culture of his time that he accepted implicitly the defamation of his own character and was more firmly convinced of his own inferiority than were those who charged him thus."[29] Some blacks he talks to do not believe in an integrated union, others believe that they never will benefit from unionization, some say the union is just a racket, and others simply ask what is in it for them (an ironic question for Lee to deal with, because it is his own).

Lee's naïveté is apparent when he goes to call on Lester McKinley, a worker at Comstock but once a Latin professor in Georgia. McKinley is suffering from homicidal mania and has been for years; he wants to kill a white man—and Lee figures in his plans. Lester had fled Georgia for fear of carrying out his obsession. He went to Albany, New York, where he consulted a psychoanalyst who told him that the homicidal mania was a consequence of Lester's overwhelming sense of racial inferiority. He recommended that what Lester should do to overcome the psychosis of race is to marry and have children by a white woman. Lester did just that, but still he was not cured. "He had become convinced," Himes writes, "that the analyst, even while prescribing for his cure, had known that in this society there was no cure. He had become certain that the analyst had known beyond all doubt that over the centuries of oppression—an oppression of body, spirit, and soul so complete that no one had ever plumbed its depths; an oppression composed of abuses that had completely destroyed the moral fiber of an entire people, abuses to the innate structure of character and spirit so brutal that their effect was inheritable like syphilis—the Negroes of America had actually become an inferior people."[31] Lester has concluded that he is insane because of his heritage of oppression and that there is nothing to do but carry out the logic of his impulses: he intends to murder Louis Foster. His plan is to join the union, become a volunteer organizer, pass out literature in the shop, provoke Foster into slapping him during an inspection tour, and then hit him with a ballpeen hammer. It would appear to be a case of temporary insanity, the union would support him, and even if he did not escape the electric chair, he would be a martyr. Lester intends to use Lee to become a volunteer organizer, and he cunningly convinces Lee of his loyalty to the union and points out the antagonism of Foster toward the labor movement as well as mentioning Foster's violent temper. Lee is taken in.

Luther McKinley is the most extreme representative of a personality type that appears again and again in Himes—the black man not only dehumanized but literally driven out of his mind by the society in which he has had to live. To a certain extent, all of Himes's protagonists are somewhat like Lester, but Lester goes the limit, admitting his insanity and coolly plotting a private act of revenge. But is Lester correct? Has the moral fiber of his race been completely destroyed? Is he justified in his desperation? The answer is found in the development Lee Gordon goes through, for Lee shares many of Lester's impulses, lacking Lester's crazed clarity only because his despair has not yet become so deep.

Lee's development moves to another stage the next Saturday when he is invited to a party at Luther's home. Ruth does not want to go, so Lee shows up alone. He meets Mollie, Luther's white mistress, a wealthy, middle-aged woman who makes fun of Luther's Marxism while supporting him. It is, Lee finds out, no ordinary party; there is a charge for each drink and the money is going to be sent to Russia. Lee pays his cash anyway, starts to get drunk, and begins to argue with the other guests, rejecting the party line on every point, especially the thesis that "the Negro problem" is indivisible from the problem of the masses. Most of the communists Lee talks to are drunken, incoherent parroters of Stalinist rhetoric, but Lee meets two party members who are to have considerable influence on him—a short, bald-headed Jew named Abe Rosenberg and a blond girl named Jackie Forks. At the end of the night, Jackie takes Lee home with her.

Lee suspects that Jackie has been assigned to him by the party, and he is repelled by her confession that he is the first black man she has kissed, but he is drawn to her nonetheless. His suspicions are correct; Jackie is trying to radicalize him. To underscore the party attitude toward the Negro problem, she reads excerpts to him from the farewell speech of a white southern officer, Lieutenant Colonel Noel F. Parrish, to the all-black 99th Pursuit Squadron. Parrish tells them they have a double responsibility—to their own race and to all mankind. Lee knows, has known for years, about the first responsibility, but he cannot accept what the Lieutenant Colonel says about the second, that "The fate of all of us is bound up with the fate of humanity, and the most important of all—*men*. No one can ask more than that you acquit yourselves like men."[32] Lee does not want to listen; he only wants to make love to Jackie. But she resists, accusing him of trying to rape her. Again it is the ritual scene a black protagonist must go through, and Lee has to leave. When he gets home, he wants to talk to Ruth and explain what happened to him the night before,

but she tells him she has to work that Sunday, and he
is left alone to think over the words of Parrish and
wonder if they have any meaning for him. He soon
finds out that they do.

He goes to the union hall for an organizational
meeting and is met by five black workers who are loud
and uncouth and who insist that he have a drink with
them in the taproom. Their dialect dominates the noise
in the bar, and the white patrons start staring at them.
Lee is ashamed—he has trouble even assuming the
first part of the double responsibility outlined by Parrish. When they go into the meeting hall, Lee sees
Lester sitting by himself off to one side and goes to
join him rather than sitting up on the platform with
the leaders. Here he fails to assume the second part of
his responsibility—his role as an official in an organization ostensibly devoted to the betterment of all mankind. The five blacks from the taproom follow him and
he realizes that he has made a foolish mistake—he has
unintentionally segregated the meeting. Before he can
act, one of the blacks asks the chairman why Lee is
not allowed up on the platform, and it is only with
difficulty that Smitty can convince them that the union
is not jim-crowed. Lee is responsible for a racial incident, one that need not have happened had he only
realized that at that moment and in that place he
should have known the extent to which his fate is
bound up with the fate of humanity.

Afterwards, Smitty takes Lee aside and berates
him for the mistake. Lee tries to counter by explaining
the black view of unionism. The union offers equality,
but because of being so accustomed to discrimination
and realizing that he must actually work harder than a
white man and earn more money to be considered
equal, the black man has come to regard equality as

meaning special privilege, being more than equal. But he cannot quite make Smitty understand.

The next day at noon he finds Rosenberg waiting for him outside the union shack. They go to lunch and over martinis get into a discussion about Jews and blacks in the United States that constitutes another of the dialogues that structure the novel. Lee begins by expressing a standard basis of resentment as far as the attitudes of blacks toward Jews are concerned—that Jews often are the landlords and merchants in the black ghettoes. Blacks are especially offended, Lee explains, because while they expect to be oppressed by white gentiles, they do not expect to be oppressed by the Jews, who are themselves an oppressed minority. Lee also says he dislikes the way Jews bring up their children and the way Jewish mothers worship their sons. Nor does he like the Jewish way of handling money. Rosenberg counters by arguing that there are few Jews in big business and that the Jewish emphasis on self-preservation that sometimes show up in their dealings with blacks is the result of nineteen hundred years of oppression. That may be so, Lee agrees, but he dislikes the stamp of oppression in the Jews as much as he does in himself and his own race. Rosenberg tells him of the Marxist idea that out of oppression can come a new way of life and that out of Negro oppression communism could come to the United States. Lee is not convinced, but his anti-Semitism is tempered as much by Rosenberg's personality as by Rosenberg's statement that "the Negro has greater enemies than the Jew can ever be."[33] Lee Gordon encounters one of those enemies the next Sunday.

Foster has invited Lee and Ruth for dinner and sends his limousine to pick them up. After dinner, Foster, a fierce hater of Roosevelt, communism, unionism, and liberalism of any kind, offers Lee a job in the personnel department at Comstock; the salary is an incredible $5,000 a year. Lee is tempted. Ruth could quit her job and for the first time he could support her and feel like a real husband. But the dialogues have had an impact; he refuses to be bought off. Ruth has to admire his integrity, but she is disappointed in the refusal; to her, the refusal indicates his lack of love. When they get home, he asks her to quit her job and depend on him anyway, but she refuses. He reflects: "It was only the white man's desire to deride the Negro man that had started the lies and propaganda about the nobility and sacrifices of Negro women in the first place."[34] He walks out, goes to Jackie's, and sleeps with her.

When he gets to the plant on Monday, he finds that the organizing campaign is in chaos because of a rumor that the organizers had sold out, that Foster has bought somebody off. Smitty hopes it will blow over by Tuesday, but it does not.

The next day, while on their way to San Pedro to pick up a sound truck, Lee and Luther are pulled over by a county sheriff's patrol car. Four deputies, all under Foster's control, get out. Their leader, Paul Dixon, asks Lee how much money he wants to betray the union. Lee says not for $100,000. They tell him that he might as well take whatever money they offer because Luther has already gotten $100. Luther admits it but, his pride hurt, claims it was $500. Lee, despite his surprise, still refuses, and the deputies pistol-whip him. Luther takes Lee to the hospital and tells him that he took the money but that he had no intention of double-crossing the union. Lee says he will tell what he knows anyway. When Joe, Smitty, and the union lawyer get to the hospital, Luther denies Lee's story, saying that Lee cursed the deputies and they jumped on him. Smitty believes Lee but he is reluctant to get into a fight with the communists. He tells Lee to forget about what happened; the organizing drive is in enough trouble as it is.

Lee goes home and tries to talk to Ruth. In his despair he decides to simply be for himself, to believe in money, black cowardice, and white hypocrisy. He is only confirmed in his feeling when he goes with Smitty and the lawyer to the sheriff's office and learns that the sheriff has an alibi for each of his men and that he will not cooperate. Smitty says that the whole business must be dropped. Lee goes to Jackie's and she believes his story, but she excuses Luther by pointing out that Marxist ethics are not the same as those of bourgeois society. Jackie does not realize that she will soon experience those ethics in action.

Party officials have received a directive to kill the betrayal rumors and proclaim Luther's innocence. The decision is made to sacrifice Jackie—her loss would be easier to take than Luther's, and to accuse Luther would be to accuse his race, something the party could not risk because it is in enough trouble with its black sympathizers as it is. Jackie is accused at the next union meeting. Lee rises and says she is being framed, that Luther is the real offender, but he is shouted down. Too many people know that Lee and Jackie are lovers. Lee quits and goes home.

The following day he moves in with Jackie and they spend almost a week together. But on the sixth night, Ruth calls and threatens to arrive with the police if Lee does not come home. He returns to Ruth, tells her he loves Jackie, packs a bag, and leaves. But Jackie will not let him stay with her; she is afraid that Ruth, whom she envisions as the archetypally jealous black woman, will come after her with a knife. She is also afraid of the humiliation she will feel at the public

condemnation of her for breaking up a Negro marriage. Lee checks into a skid-row hotel.

Lee thinks he has no pride left. He has been defeated on all counts. At eight the next morning he goes
to Foster's office. When Foster finally decides to see
him at eleven, Lee says he will take the job in the
personnel office. Foster tells him the job no longer
exists.

So when Luther calls for him and asks if he would
like to make some money, Lee sees no reason to refuse.
They drive to the bungalow of Paul Dixon, the sheriff's
deputy. Dixon shows them a stack of $100 bills, gives
them each one, and says he will have a job for them in
a few days. Luther hesitates, saying he wants more
money. When Paul turns his back on them to get some
beer from the refrigerator, Luther pulls out a switchblade knife and stabs him to death. Luther orders Lee
to wipe away all fingerprints, takes the money, and he
and Lee go back to Luther's house. Lee refuses to
accept any of the money. Luther argues with him in
yet another dialogue, saying that Paul is only a "peck-
erwood," that killing a white man is, for a black man, a
natural act, not a murder. All kinds of wars are going
on, Luther says, in an echo of *If He Hollers Let Him
Go*, and that as a black man he has to fight everybody.
He is a communist, but he is a black before that, and
above all he is looking out for himself. As far as he is
concerned both the party and Foster are using him in
the same way and both because he is black. "I knows
how to be a nigger and make it pay," he says.[35]

Lee leaves, realizing that Luther is a man without
a soul and that he very nearly lost his own. He goes to
Jackie and tells her what happened and asks her to
give him an alibi. She asks him to leave; she just cannot lie for him. When he stretches out on the couch
and falls asleep, she calls the police. He is grilled at

headquarters but will not talk. He is beaten unconscious with a leaded hose. Luther is shot to death re-
sisting arrest, Lee learns later.

But if Jackie is not willing to support him, the
union is. Smitty and the lawyer get Lee out on a writ
of habeas corpus by persuading some union members
to sign alibis covering for him. Even when Smitty finds
out the truth from Lee, that Lee had indeed gone to
Dixon's for money, he refuses to give up on him. He
says he will give Lee one more chance. If Lee can get
the black vote for the election, the union will back him
in court (and Lee had better hope that no evidence
placing him at the scene of the crime turns up). If not,
he will be dropped. He has six days.

At home, Ruth tells him she has quit her job as he
has requested for so long. She is willing to trust him;
he, in turn, tells her that he did not love Jackie. But he
knows he cannot move back in with Ruth until he
proves himself. He goes back to his hotel, and there
admits to himself, for the first time in his life, that "he
could not excuse his predicament on grounds of race.
This time he alone was to blame—Lee Gordon, a
human being, one of the cheap, weak people of the
world."[36]

Smitty has prepared a press release on Lee's arrest
making Lee out to be a martyr, but Foster has acted to
short-circuit whatever advantage Lee might have. Foster has announced hiring a black in the personnel department and the promotion of two blacks to leader-
men. Lee gets nowhere the first day; most black
workers cannot see what the union will give them that
Foster has not already promised. The second day Lee
works hard but gets only two recruits. That night he
thinks of Parrish's speech, and he knows that what he
must do, what he should have been trying to do all
along, is to acquit himself as a man. But how is he to

do it? The pre-election meeting is a failure, and Lee feels he is not doing his job. But Smitty keeps him going. The union wants to organize blacks from the community to parade in support of the recruitment drive. He calls ministers, the heads of welfare agencies, and others, but he gets nowhere. He has come down with a bad cold and is convinced that he is sinking into defeat. It is in that condition in his squalid hotel room that Rosenberg finds him the night before the election.

Rosenberg, in the final dialogue of the novel, gives a powerful explanation of why he still believes in communism even though he has been expelled from the party because of his refusal to go along with the denunciation of Jackie. Lee, in contrast, can only confess that he tried to sell the union out. Rosenberg drops the Marxist rhetoric and addresses Lee's problem directly: "Lee, you must face it, friend. You may die for the murder of Paul Dixon, but once you resolve your indecision toward life and embrace your own reality, you will not be afraid to die."[37] Lee's dilemma has not simply been that he is black, that he has resented being supported by his wife, or that he has been self-centered; it is that he has never embraced his reality, he has never, as the Lieutenant Colonel emphasized, accepted his double responsibility. Until he does that he can never acquit himself as a man.

Lee wakes to sunshine, as if he has gone through a religious conversion. He is buoyant as he rides to the plant (a ride that contrasts with the vicious, tire-screeching, hate-filled ride that Bob Jones has that first morning in *If He Hollers Let Him Go*) and he looks upon everything with a new kind of vision: "Now he saw the city that he had never seen, though it had been ten thousand times within his eyes—the pleasant little shops on Fifth Street toward the Square, sunlight on the buildings—delicate pastel tracings against the blue—and two wedding gowns in a shop window like petals of eternal hope; and the faces of the people of the race—the human race—each with its story of the crusade."[38]

When he gets to the plant, he sees a line of deputy sheriffs blocking off the street by the union shack. He sees the union sound truck and is motioned inside by Joe Ptak. Smitty tells him that a warrant has been issued for Lee's arrest and that they want him to stay out of sight because of the affidavits. Again, Lee feels that he is nothing but trouble, that he may have cost the union Comstock, perhaps California itself. He watches as Joe and a squad of workers try to break the deputies' line and he wonders about what he could do for those who had befriended him, what he could do for Rosenberg, for Smitty, for Ruth, for the union itself. He sees Joe move forward with the union banner, the workers behind him, but they are all driven back by the deputies' clubs, all that is except Joe. He stands his ground until he is knocked down. As Joe falls, Lee sees Ruth and Rosenberg in the crowd and senses that time is running out. He jumps from the truck, fights his way to Joe, picks up the banner and marches down the street.

What Lee's final action represents is an existential solution to the human—and by inclusion, the racial—problem. Like Sartre, Himes seems to maintain in *Lonely Crusade* that human nature is fixed only in the same sense that men have agreed to recognize certain attributes of human nature; this nature may be changed if men merely agree on different attributes, or even if one man courageously acts in contradiction to the principles as ordinarily accepted. And this is what Lee does in picking up the banner, an act that is necessitated by the step-by-step education he has received through his dialogues with Smitty, Joe, the communists at Luther's party, Luther himself, Jackie, Foster, and Rosenberg. What the dialogues have done is to help Lee overcome the self-concepts he has acquired as a black man and, like Orestes in Sartre's *Le Sursis*, change his character by an act of will. Lee ends like yet another Sartrean hero, Mathieu in *La Mort dans l' Âme*, who becomes infuriated at his own sense of helplessness the day before the armistice is to be signed between France and Germany in 1940 and joins a platoon of combat troops who are about to put up a last-ditch fight against the occupation of a small town. Hidden in a belfry, he fires at the German troops until he is brought down by grenades. He has at last taken action against the forces that seek to enslave him. Lee's redemption is of the same type. Himes suggests that active struggle is the only course open to a man tormented by destiny and that the struggle itself is a retort—man wins the victory simply by refusing to capitulate. Cooperation in group action becomes a sort of salvation.

Of course, what Lee is struggling against is not defined any better, despite the series of dialogues, than is the disease Rieux struggles against in Camus's *La Peste*. What, after all, is the ultimate cause of racial tension in the United States? When the problem lessens, perhaps Lee will know no more about it than when he began, just as Rieux knows no more about the plague; but he will feel that the struggle has been worthwhile. The crusade is by necessity a lonely one because it is an existential one.

Unfortunately, *Lonely Crusade* was not easily understood when it appeared, perhaps because the ideas Himes develops were so unfamiliar to many of his readers. One reviewer, for instance, stated that the diagnosis of "the Negro problem" Himes makes "reveals a racial malady for which there is no immediate remedy."[39] Yet, as we have seen, Lee's assumption of the union banner, is, at least in the sense of what the act means to Lee as a black man, an immediate solution of sorts. It is not the final solution, certainly not the only solution, but it is a positive answer to what is usually simply a negative question. Another reviewer saw Lee as a tragic figure, caught in a growing despair over being black and hamstrung in all his human relationships.[40] But at the end of the novel quite the opposite is true. A third reviewer, apparently neglecting Lee's lunchtime dialogue with Rosenberg, emphasized the anti-Semitism in the novel: "The point that Mr. Himes drives home quite well is that the majority of Negroes . . . tend to give vent to expressions that by sound and fury are anti-Semitic. A closer reading of this book might suggest that Negroes are fed up with the prattle about the unity of all minority groups."[41] On the contrary, a closer reading reveals that one of the major themes in the novel derives from the word union *with* its implications of the unity of mankind.

Even the attacks on the novel by Marxist critics seem at least a little unfair. Himes does make individual communists appear ridiculous at Luther's party and he does emphasize his dislike for the ruthlessness of party policy and the hypocrisy that often creeps into the Marxist interpretation of ethics; but through Rosenberg, Himes allows Marxist theory to be presented clearly and at times forcefully. It is apparent that Himes is not a communist and there is little indication that Lee could ever become one, but the reasons for Rosenberg's commitment are apparent and understandable. What Himes objects to most is not communism as such, but the failure of the party to carry out the humanitarian side of its program in a consistent way. It is one thing to want the organizing drive to succeed; it is another thing to frame Jackie Forks in order to make it succeed. An individual can sacrifice himself for the many; it is wrong for the many to sacrifice an individual for the good of the group. This is what Himes is getting at in his representation of the Communist Party in *Lonely Crusade*.

There are problems, however, with the structure of the novel. In his justifiable attempt to suggest the scope and complexities of union organizing, Himes introduces a large number of characters and subplots. Lester McKinley, for example, is one of the most memorable minor characters in the novel, but his somewhat elaborate plot to murder Foster goes nowhere too quickly. And Ruth, a character who should be major, never quite comes to life; in addition, she has, as one reviewer wrote, "all the connotations of a dumb Nelly."[42] Part of the problem perhaps stems from Himes's omniscient point of view. He shifts back and forth from character to character and Lee's consciousness is not allowed to dominate the story the way it might. The result is an occasionally awkward drop in the intensity of the story, especially when Himes uses flashbacks to give us Lee's history.

But even though the novel is crammed with characters and events, it leaves the reader with an impression of power. The sudden turns of plot are a Himes trademark, and while they again brought the charge of melodrama from the reviewers, they do contribute an overwhelming sense of the rush of events that makes Lee's final action seem all the more heroic. The plot is, of course, punctuated by the dialogues which are in themselves handled well. A novel of ideas is not easy to write without turning it into an illustrated lecture, but Himes avoids this through a combination of realistic reproduction of speech patterns and keeping the reader aware of the setting in which the dialogue is taking place. In the dialogue at Luther's party, for instance, Himes never lets the reader forget that drinking, music, and partying are going on at the same time that Lee is hearing about an article in *The Daily World*.

Then, too, the larger setting—Los Angeles in the midst of World War II—is described fully, making *Lonely Crusade* a companion volume to *If He Hollers Let Him Go* as social history. We get not only the appearance of the war plants and the image of the sprawling city, but we get the mood of the workers, who are making big money for the first time, contrasted with the concerns of the organizers, who are worrying about what will happen when the war ends. We get an insightful picture of the relationship between unionization and communist activities during the time. And we get, once again in Lee's desperately shouted welcome to the Japanese planes, an attitude toward the war effort that is little remembered. Like *If He Hollers Let Him Go*, *Lonely Crusade* bears consideration as a war novel—its title indicates as much.

In his first two novels, Himes thus moves from racial outrage toward a vigorous resolution that in no way actually diminishes his anger. The war Bob Jones declares is fought on a different level and in a different way by Lee Gordon, but it is not won. What makes Bob's story such a sad and frustrating one is that while he thinks he recognizes the enemy and is willing to fight, he does not know how to draw the lines of battle. Lee Gordon is not entirely certain who the enemy is and realizes that his worst enemy is perhaps himself, but he has learned the meaning of struggle and at the end he knows how to fight. He still possesses the angry consciousness of the Himes hero but he has been transformed through existential commitment into a symbol of change, hope, and resolution. That Himes, in his subsequent work, moves away from the heroics with which Lee's story concludes does diminish *Lonely Crusade* as a statement of optimism concerning race relations in the United States; but it does not diminish Lee himself as a character and the ideas he represents through his actions.

"Something
to Hate Me For":
The Confessional Novels

"Into the furnace let me go alone. . . ."
—*Claude McKay*, "Baptism"

With *Cast the First Stone*, Himes moves, for reasons that were more practical than ideological, momentarily away from the racially charged novels he had written in *If He Hollers Let Him Go* and *Lonely Crusade* and into what Robert Bone terms the assimilationist novel, in which black writers deal with white characters and white problems. "Reasoning by simple analogy, the assimilationists argued that Negroes were at last breaking out of their ghettoes and moving toward full participation in every phase of American life," Bone explains. "Why not art? Let the Negro novelist demonstrate his cosmopolitanism by writing of the dominant majority."[1] Exploring the possibilities in "integrated art" were Willard Motley with *Knock on Any Door* (1947) and *We Fished All Night* (1950), Zora Neale Huston with *Seraph on the Suwanee* (1948), William Gardner Smith with *Anger at Innocence* (1950), and Ann Petry with *Country Place* (1947). *Knock on Any Door*, for example, is concerned with Italian immigrants in Chicago, and *Seraph on the Suwanee* has as its central character an impoverished white woman in the rural South. These novels seem to have been written to at least partially demonstrate that the black artist is ready for integration. And there was the feeling (on the part of publishers at any rate) that the material on which the novels produced by the Wright school had been based was exhausted—or that readers were growing tired of the ragingly depressing narratives that were inspired by *Native Son*. The integrationist novel also seemed to offer a broader scope for black writers, many of whom felt restricted in their art by the unrelenting theme of protest that had come to be expected from them.

In choosing a white protagonist and eliminating almost all suggestion of racial tension in *Cast the First Stone*, Himes was not motivated by quite the same reasons that some of the other writers who produced integrationist novels in the years after World War II were. *Cast the First Stone*, which derives from Himes's prison experiences, was first written as *Black Sheep* and was not an assimilationist novel at all. After nearly a decade of trying to get the novel published, and receiving some advice from a publisher that the market for books about young, oppressed black men was not good, Himes revised the novel by changing the race of the central character and, consequently, that of many of the minor characters as well. The story itself remained essentially the same, however. That the changes Himes effected made *Black Sheep* publishable as *Cast the First Stone* is itself a commentary on race relations in the United States at the time.

Cast the First Stone is actually two books in one. The first part is a conventional prison novel—actually not so much a novel as a day-by-day account of prison life with descriptions of bedbug-infested cells, homicidal convicts, sadistic guards, sickening food, and the inevitable riot. The novel is ordinary in this respect and the prison scenes are occasionally reminiscent of

those in *An American Tragedy* by Dreiser, and they
point toward such later novels as Frank Eli's *The Riot*.
Himes's depiction of life within the walls is powerfully
graphic, however, and many memorable passages,
such as Jim Monroe's description of what it is like to
awaken in a bunk in the state penitentiary, emerge:
"On awakening each morning I had my choice of looking at the convicts dress in their grayed and sweat-
stiffened socks which they wore from week to week
and their bagged stinking trousers which they wore
from year to year, and their gaunt and patched coats
which the officials seemed to think never wore out; or
I could look underneath the sagging upper mattresses
out of the west windows at the back of the hospital,
weather-stained and still asleep, housing tuberculosis
and syphilis and cuts and lacerations and contusions
and infections and operations and skulls cracked by
guards' stocks, and death."[2] But the second part of the
novel deals with a bizarre love affair between Jim
Monroe and a youngster named Dido who is moved
into his cellblock. This treatment of homosexual love,
which disturbed several reviewers and which may still
be troubling to certain readers, builds toward a disappointment for Jim and Dido that is made all the more
believable by the way Himes shows the subtle changes
that Jim Monroe has gone through after years of living
in an all-male environment.

　　Jim Monroe (prisoner number 109130) is sentenced to a prison (never named in the novel) for
twenty to twenty-five years. Armed robbery. In his
first walk around the coal-company dormitory to
which he is assigned, Jim is approached by a convict
who offers him a pack of cigarettes in exchange for an
unmentioned but plainly suggested relationship. Jim
backs off; he has been in jail before and he under-
stands the con-or-be-conned rule of life. He soon

meets Mal Streator, who has served five years already for first-degree murder. Mal shows Jim around, explains the system to him, and the two become close friends. Never comfortable living a regimented life, Jim must adjust to monotonous food (breakfasts of soupy oatmeal and one link of fried sausage in congealed grease), the menial duties of his work assignment as a porter, and the constant problem of living under the eyes of the guards: Fletcher, who once shot a convict to death from outside a locked cell; Cody, a quiet man who never repeated an order (but when he started to run, everyone knew a convict was going to die); and the others. All of this must be endured in an institution built to hold eighteen hundred inmates and now holding four thousand.

Jim finds himself strangely affected by his relationship with Mal, who makes a show of rejecting homosexuality. But the denial of women, the very atmosphere of prison—both have an odd influence on a man. One night Jim and Mal sit on Mal's bunk and start to talk about the women they had known. "We kept talking about it until every time we'd accidentally touch each other we'd feel a shock," Jim remembers. "I was startled at the femininity a man's face could assume when you're looking at it warmly and passionately, and off to yourselves in prison where there are all men and there is no comparison."[3] This relationship with Mal, which foreshadows the later involvement with Dido, is interrupted when Mal is transferred the next day to a new job.

After Mal leaves, Jim gets into trouble for refusing to obey work orders and is assigned to push a wheelbarrow as a regular member of the coal company. His subsequent refusal to wheel coal gets him thrown into the correction cells—the hole. He is put into a cell with three others and the lights are turned off. There are only scraps of blankets for Jim and his companions to use against the cold and they spend the night huddling together trying not to think about the bedbugs that are biting them. The next morning when asked if he is ready to go to work, Jim goes.

He moves from assignment to assignment in the prison—from sweeping the wheelbarrow tracks to schoolteacher (fired during the first day for not knowing what a predicate adjective is), to pupil, to the soup company, and in and out of the hospital. For awhile his major duty (and by far his most profitable) is running a poker game (using a carefully marked deck) with a prisoner named Blocker. Jim becomes one of the gambling lords in the penitentiary, but he begins to lose interest in the poker racket when he signs up for a $500 law course and starts studying. At the same time another prisoner interests him in doing some writing, and Jim's development into a hardened convict ends.

As his adjustment to prison life proceeds, Jim witnesses and lives through several traumatic scenes. There is the riot when five hundred convicts with two guns they had obtained by attacking the guards in the idle room rush the door only to back down when they see one official, Cody, walking toward them. Without saying a word, he disarms the men with the pistols, and then shoots (five times) another convict who had gone crazy from the strain and started screaming. There is the pathetic scene when Jim's broken-down and worried mother comes to visit him. There is the night when the prisoners sit around to await the execution of Doctor Snodgrass, a prominent surgeon, who had killed his girl friend to keep his wife from finding out about his affair. There are the breaks and the attempted breaks. And there is the fire that starts in the 10 & 11 block and sweeps through much of the prison,

roasting dozens of convicts in their cells, leading to
widespread rioting and looting among the survivors,
and necessitating the calling out of the national guard.
One benefit is that the investigation that follows even-
tuates in improved conditions and the reduction of
sentences to the statutory minimums with time off for
good behavior—thus reducing Jim's sentence by thir-
teen years and seven months.

Along with the scenes that Jim witnesses, his education is furthered by the characters he meets inside
the prison walls, where in an environment of enforced
conformity, normalcy is impossible. There is Starlight,
short, fat, and redheaded, who claimed that he was a
member of the syndicate, that he carried the nickname
of the Boston Red Squirrel, and that he had been General MacArthur's orderly during the war. There is
Blackie, machine gunner for the Lucky Lou gang,
doing double life for a multiple murder in Blackstone
Park. There is doll-like Bobby Guy who sexually tor-
ments the entire cell block. And there is Metz, who
interests Jim in short-story writing. Metz was part
owner of a jewelry store and he had been leading a
comfortable life until one night he saw his wife riding
in a taxi with another man. He went searching for her
with a pistol. He found his wife and her boy friend
getting into another taxi in front of a restaurant, had
his driver catch up with them, and he leaned out the
window of his taxi and shot the woman. In prison,
Metz is a controlled and philosophical man. But the
most important fellow-prisoner Jim meets, as far as his
own development as a character is concerned, is Dido.

Duke Dido, wearing a ukelele on a cord around
his neck, is brought to Jim's section one Saturday
morning. He has a longish jaw, full lips, and "a throat
as lovely as a woman's."[4] Jim, because he has just
written his letter to the governor asking for a pardon

and must avoid trouble of all sorts, meets Dido at a
dangerous time. They become close friends, so close
that the other convicts start kidding them—at first not
seriously. But as Jim and Dido continue to read aloud
to one another, as they stand at the window together
and watch the sunset, and as they do such things as sit
up all night together on Christmas eve, the talk about
them increases. Jim learns that Dido had done a year
on a chain gang in Florida for grand larceny, that he
had been a hobo and had broken both kneecaps when
he was pushed from a moving train, that he had been
a deserter from the army, and that he had spent some
time in an insane asylum. But what disturbs Jim the
most is to learn that Dido had worked in cabarets as a
female impersonator. Despite his affection for Dido,
despite the impulses that years in prison without
women had given him, he cannot quite accept the idea
of becoming Dido's lover. The pressure builds after
Jim has learned that the governor is going to commute
his sentence and that he will be eligible for parole in
September. One night Dido hands him a typewritten
note begging for consummation. Jim is disgusted, and
Dido threatens to kill himself—but Dido is unable to
carry out his threat that night.

Jim and Dido cannot get along the same thereafter, but the whispering campaign against them
builds nonetheless. A friendly guard warns Jim that
complaints have reached the warden that Jim and
Dido are carrying on too openly, so much so that it is
offensive to the other convicts. Jim still has too much
anger and pride to allow his life to be dictated by
what others think; and out of defiance, he continues to
be as friendly to Dido as ever. They continue to read
to one another, even going so far as to stretch out on
the same bunk. The guard, who does not want to see
Jim lose his chance for early parole, tries to get rid of

Dido by writing him up for sexual perversion. Jim
goes to the guard stand and insists that he be written
up too. Both of them are sent to the hole for five days
and Jim loses his commutation. When they get out
they are assigned separate cells in the "girl-boy" company for sexual perverts.

Jim's mother has heard about the charges and insists on an investigation. Jim is cleared but not Dido,
which means that they will be separated (Jim is assigned to the prison farm). On the evening before Jim
is to leave the company, he stops by Dido's cell to say
goodbye. "He leaned forward and I kissed him" Jim
says, "It was the first and only time I had ever kissed
him. There was no passion in the kiss but it had a
great tenderness. A couple of guys passing on the
range made kissing sounds but we didn't care."[5] That
night Dido hangs himself in his cell, and after the
cellblock quiets down and his own grief levels out, Jim
realizes that Dido had committed suicide to give him a
perfect ending: "It was so much like him to do this
one irrevocable thing to let me know for always that I
was the only one."[6] The next morning when he gets on
the truck to leave for the farm, he looks back at the
prison walls and realizes that he has come out a win-
ner of sorts; and he knows that he is on the way to
freedom.

Cast the First Stone is more than just a novel of
prison life (although it succeeds simply as that); it is
also a frank and illuminating treatment of love between men. Despite occasional weaknesses in dialogue
(especially when Jim calls Dido "sweet boy" and Dido
refers to Jim as "Puggy Wuggy"), ritual scenes that
are overdone (mother visiting the young convict, for
instance), and an ending that is almost too abrupt
even in a Himes novel, the book, in its depiction of
Jim's relationship with Dido, demonstrates Himes's
considerable range in characterization.

When the novel appeared, it was praised for its competence, its intensity, and its accuracy; but several reviewers were apparently greatly disturbed by the love scenes. "This is a very odd book," W. R. Burnett wrote in the *Saturday Review of Literature*. "For two-thirds of the book we have none of the esthetic generalization of a novel, but instead the unrelieved particularity of factual writing. . . . But the oddest thing of all is the preoccupation with homosexuality. . . . I'll admit that I'm prejudiced and that prejudice makes for false judgments. So I will conclude by saying that the account of this love affair is highly original—I've never read anything like it—and for that reason alone is perhaps worth the reader's while. You—readers and book-buyers—will have to be the judge."[7] Burnett is, of course, right in saying that there is not another like it and in mirroring a reaction that the novel elicited from many readers—and still does. But Americans, as Leslie Fiedler has pointed out in *Love and Death in the American Novel*, have never been able to treat openly or accept the kind of tension that builds between Jim and Dido, even if it is prefigured much less clearly in the *Leatherstocking Tales* (Natty Bumppo and Chingachgook), *Moby Dick* (Ishmael and Queequeg), *Huckleberry Finn* (Huck and Jim), and many other lesser novels. And this tension is handled by Himes with a bruising kind of honesty. As Frederic Morton commented in the *New York Herald Tribune Book Review*, "Mr. Himes seems to have pounded his typewriter with brass knuckles without losing either accuracy or aim. He has succeeded twice: in recreating the inferno of a penitentiary; and in recording the ordeal of a convict's emotional growth."[8]

It is his own emotional growth that Himes turns to in his next published novel, *The Third Generation* (1954), but this time more directly, beginning with the primal basis of his development. Through a series of traumatic scenes that structure the novel like the dialogues in *Lonely Crusade*, Himes writes about the disintegration of a family only thinly disguised from his own, a family that is torn apart by racial tension, a burden of ancestral guilt, and psychological conflict. The young protagonist of the story, Charles Taylor, emerges as a survivor at the end, redeemed somewhat by his suffering as the earlier Himes heroes are, but just barely. What is impressive to the reader, despite the horrifying and often sickening process it involves, is the way Himes, through the autobiographical Charles, exorcises himself of one of his private demons and comes to understand the impulse behind his own self-destructive urges.

The Third Generation began to take shape when Himes, while visiting his brother Joe in 1950 at North Carolina College, looked over the notes his mother had made in starting to trace the history of her half-white family. He did not use her material, but he started to think about the implications of his own family history on himself and his intense love for his mother, who had died before his first novel was published. The result is a chronicle that derives its title and one of its central themes from Exodus 20:5: "for I the Lord thy God am a jealous God, visiting the iniquity of the fathers upon the children unto the third and fourth generation of them that hate me." The burden of sin and guilt arising out of a heritage of slavery, conflicting attitudes toward miscegenation, and sexual maladjustment compounded by racial tension is documented, analyzed, and ultimately laid to rest by Himes as he works his way through the childhood, adolescence, and young manhood of Charles Taylor.

Charles is three years old when the novel opens. His father, Professor Taylor, his mother, and his two brothers, William (five) and Thomas (eleven), are living in a house his father rents from the president of the college where he teaches. Mrs. Taylor, a small, proud, light-skinned woman who has never quite recovered from having Charles, is resentful that any of her children resemble her short, dark husband, with whom she is openly disappointed because he is too submissive to others, too ingratiating to please her and her fierce pride. She liked Charles the best because he was the lightest in color of her children. "She had been reared," writes Himes, "in the tradition that Negroes with straight hair and light complexions were superior to dark complexioned Negroes with kinky hair."[9] This belief, which is an obsession with her, is a constant source of trouble in her marriage and perverts her relationship with her children and with Charles especially.

Mrs. Taylor singles Charles out from the beginning. She tries, for example, to keep his hair straight by massaging his scalp with olive oil and giving it one hundred brush strokes daily. And she reminds him of his white-blooded ancestry on her side of the family as if it, not the African heritage of his father's side, is what he must live up to. She tried to pass on to Charles the childhood fantasy that she was descended from an English nobleman, a fantasy she had revived out of the disillusionment of her marriage. She even went so far as to claim that she possessed only one thirty-second Negro blood. Her husband dislikes what she is doing to Charles and accuses her, among other things, of trying to make a girl out of her son. And it is true, as she admits to herself, that she had wanted a girl when Charles was born. Charles, as a consequence, grows up with a double burden—the psychologically destructive racial attitudes of his mother, and the classically disturbing problem of sexual identification imposed on him by her.

With her consciousness of her light skin and her

hatred of segregation, Mrs. Taylor is especially disturbed when her husband gets a new job at a college in Mississippi. But Professor Taylor likes his work and the children are happy in the rural setting. It is there, however, that Charles witnesses the first of several traumatic scenes that are to shape his life. He sees a young college girl crushed by a wagon. He faints and his father carries him home. Charles awakens, smothered in his mother's arms, thinking he is dead. He faints again to escape the pain and terror that have overwhelmed him. The next day his mother wants him to talk about it, but he cannot confess his feelings to her. From that point on he cannot express himself to his mother, cannot overcome the smothering effect of her presence. Instead of talking out his anxieties, he represses them. The incident only confirms his mother's hatred of Mississippi and the savage environment she thinks it is. She sends her oldest son, Tom, to Cleveland to live with relatives, and insists on instructing William and Charles at home.

Charles begins to realize that he loves and hates his mother at the same time, and he is both attracted and repelled when she lets him brush her long hair, file her nails, and massage her feet. When his mother and father quarrel, as they often do, he has the urge to cut off his father's head with an ax. He is, of course, suffering horribly from an unresolved oedipal complex, and his mother's actions seem calculated to compound his dilemma. They are also symptomatic of the frustration she feels as a woman who can pass for white yet is compelled to abide by the laws of segregation. Her resentment soon leads to trouble. She is arrested in Natchez for patronizing a white dentist. She pulls a pistol on a white farmer who refuses to let her husband's car pass the farmer's mule-drawn wagon. And finally, to get the family out of Mississippi, she goes to

Vicksburg, registers in a white hotel, and then the next morning lets it be known who she is. The governor phones Professor Taylor and tells him he has forty-eight hours to get his wife out of Mississippi. They go to St. Louis for the summer and then move to Pine Bluff, Arkansas, where Professor Taylor gets another—and, as it turns out, his last—teaching job. Despite their youth, Charles and William are enrolled at the college.

Mrs. Taylor continues to brood and worry over Charles, who becomes more and more violence-prone. Charles's behavior leads to a punishment that profoundly affects him after he experiences his second traumatic scene. He and William get interested in chemistry and the making of explosives. The two of them are asked to demonstrate what they have learned at the annual precommencement program for the parents of college students. But Charles, because of misbehavior, is forbidden to take part by his mother, who warns him that God is going to punish him for the way he acts. Charles is thus sitting in the audience when William is blinded while doing the demonstration. William is rushed to the white hospital, where he is given emergency treatment but refused admittance. He is taken to the black hospital, and it is learned that there is no realistic hope of recovery. Charles experiences "a sense of shock that never wore off," Himes emphasizes. "He might have been able to adjust to his brother's loss of sight. But he never learned to rationalize the error of God's judgment—the profound and startling knowledge that virtue didn't pay."[10] Charles is left with a sense of guilt, wondering why it was William, his happy and well-behaved brother, who is injured instead of himself.

His mother takes William to St. Louis for treatment and at the end of the summer, Professor Taylor and Charles follow her there. Professor Taylor cannot find a teaching job and becomes a waiter in a roadhouse. Charles has a rough time in high school and is fired from two jobs for stealing. Tom comes home briefly, a university graduate, fails as a real-estate salesman, disappoints his mother, and drifts away to Detroit and out of the family's life. Mrs. Taylor is left with a feeling of persecution, convinced that everyone, from her husband on down, has failed her. But she manages to conquer her paranoia for a time when her husband loses his job because of Prohibition just as they are told William needs another operation. She knows for once that she is needed, pulls the family together, and they move to Cleveland.

She does not change her arrogant ways, however, and she cannot get along with her in-laws, upon whom she and her husband are partially dependent their first months in Cleveland. Charles finds that he is but one of eight blacks attending his new high school. He is shy, unable to meet and get along with girls, and socially inept; his mother, however, continues to defend and protect him, even when he loses control of his aunt's automobile and runs it into a crowd of people waiting for a bus. When he is hauled into court, his mother insists that he is the victim and that his aunt and uncle are liable for allowing a minor to drive. The judge reprimands Charles for driving without a license and forbids him to drive again. His aunt and uncle lose their home and their savings to pay damages, but his mother keeps this information from him so he will not suffer from guilt that she thinks is needless. And instead of carrying out her moral obligation to help her in-laws sustain the costs of Charles's accident, she takes money from the sale of property in St. Louis and buys a house in a white neighborhood.

But the family is happy for a time in the pleasant

house. Professor Taylor gets a lot of carpentry work in the area, his mother relaxes in the knowledge that she is living for the first time in an unsegregated setting, and Charles is able for the first time in his life to have friends over. He loses his shyness, learns to dance, and even goes out on his first date. Outwardly he seems happily adjusted, but his adjustment is simply a matter of successful repression. He had begun putting into practice a credo he had formulated after William's accident: "No matter how hurt you are, if you don't think about it, it can't hurt."[11] But what is a successful formula for social adjustment at the time will inevitably become a formula for psychological maladjustment in the future.

Charles graduates from high school in January and in March gets a job as a busboy at an eastside hotel. The second day on the job, he falls down an elevator shaft, fracturing three vertebrae, breaking his left arm, and damaging most of his teeth. Like William after his accident, Charles is refused admittance at the first hospital and has to be taken to a hospital that admits blacks. His mother and father are caught in mutual but separate grief—his mother for pushing Charles to take the job to earn money for college, and his father for wanting Charles to experience, for the sake of discipline, some of the same work he had done. As Charles recuperates, he starts to hate the sight of his mother's grief-stricken face. She had been unsuccessful in trying to sue the hotel and had taken to hanging around the service entrance trying to get pertinent testimony from the waiters. Her husband had tried to keep her away and their fighting got worse.

Charles is released from the hospital early in July after a four-month stay. He is able to walk but must wear a cumbersome back-brace. He keeps to himself, avoids his friends, and starts taking long walks at night. His sexual urges drive him to Scovill Avenue, where he finds a prostitute, but the experience makes him fear that his accident has incapacitated him sexually. He goes to see a doctor, and after being reassured, he goes back to Scovill, gets the same girl, and stays the night this time. All summer long he returns to the bordello, and all summer long his mother waits up for him with accusing looks.

In the fall when he goes to college, he feels as if he has been relieved of a great burden as he leaves his mother behind. With his disability and the hotel salary he continues to receive, he buys a roadster and drives it about town smoking a pipe. He joins a fraternity and tries to get involved in campus life. But without his mother there to push him, he does not succeed academically. At Christmastime, he goes home and stays out night after night getting drunk. After getting back to school, he wrecks his car. His college career comes to an end when (after an altercation in a speakeasy) he is allowed to withdraw because of ill health and failing grades.

He is sick for two months when he goes home and his parents are fighting worse than ever. His father's carpentry work had fallen off and he was forced to take work as a laborer. When Charles recovers, he draws $300 from the bank and winds up in a gambling joint on Cedar Avenue. The same night he buys a powerful red car and starts running around with a girl named Peggy. But several months later when she tells him that she is pregnant, he avoids her (he has never told her where he lives), and she has to be sent back to her family in Georgia. Charles's drinking increases, and his mother tries to gain control of the hotel salary. When the manager says that he cannot allow her to do so, she accuses him of cheating Charles out of a fair settlement. The manager loses his patience with her and stops the checks entirely. The finance company comes to take his car, and rather than turn it in, Charles runs it into a concrete abutment.

Charles returns to the gambling joints and meets a small-time thief named Poker. He begins to accompany Poker on his burglary expeditions, and his mother begins to suspect what he is doing. She wants him to move out of the house, but his father insists that he stay. One morning he hears his parents struggling and finds his father choking his mother. Charles, spinning the oedipal plot further, hits Professor Taylor and comforts his mother. His father leaves the house, and his mother sues for divorce.

To get out of giving a deposition for the divorce proceedings, Charles hunts Poker up. They steal a car and drive to Columbus, where they stay at his old college boarding house. The next morning the stolen car is damaged by an expensive sedan belonging to a middle-aged white man who gives Charles $20 and tells him to come by his office the following day with the garage bill, which Charles does. He gets a check for $85 from the man, cashes it at a bank, and manages to get a sheaf of blank checks from the teller. Poker thinks they have pressed their luck far enough and goes home. He is correct; Charles is caught passing bogus checks. His bail is set at $1500, which his parents cannot raise, and he must stay in the county jail until his case is heard. The divorce goes through while he is locked up. He gets a suspended sentence—but, to the surprise and dismay of his mother, he is paroled to his father.

Professor Taylor is living in a squalid room a half block off Cedar Ave. He is working as a porter in a nightclub run by racketeers. Mrs. Taylor has sold the house and lives in a room of her own. She has dyed her hair, has started smoking cigarettes, and, as she has done all her adult life, spends much of her time squabbling, this time with her landlords.

Charles once again goes back to the gambling joints. He spends most of his time with a prostitute named Veeny, returning to his father's room only to change clothes. The prostitute, who is a symbolic counterpart to his mother, has a consuming desire that paralyzes Charles with evil. One night when he is drunk in Veeny's bed, his mother, who has enlisted his father's help, finds him there. Veeny's pimp handles Mrs. Taylor roughly in trying to get her out of the room, and Professor Taylor hits the pimp with a chair. The pimp pulls a knife, and Professor Taylor is fatally stabbed. Mrs. Taylor stays with her husband's body at the hospital, the two reconciled at last. Charles goes back to his father's room resolving to look up Peggy and his child. Although he is alone and sealed into his private horror, he feels as if a cycle has come to completion, as if whatever punishment has been due him and his family is now over. His last words to himself as he goes to sleep are "Good-bye, Mama."[12]

As autobiographical as *The Third Generation* is, Himes is clearly exorcising himself of a private demon in the novel—or, at the very least, as David Littlejohn suggests, settling some long-rankling childhood scores.[13] It is necessary when commenting on a confessional novel to ask what the author has learned to make his own experiences a fitting subject for a book; self-therapy, while valuable in itself, is usually not enough to make a novel anything more than an extension of a suicide note. But through the series of traumatic scenes—the girl being crushed by the wagon, William's accident, Charles's fall into the elevator shaft, his father choking his mother, and the stabbing of his father in Veeny's room—Himes strings together a chain of images that objectifies the theme of double guilt through racial oppression and an unresolved oedipal complex. And in the process Himes apparently learns the cause of his own self-destructive urges.

Like *Lonely Crusade*, *The Third Generation* has an upbeat ending, although an ending that is much more muted than the earlier novel. As he is lying on his father's bed, with the smell of his father still in the bedclothes, Charles turns from thinking of his own agony to a concern for Peggy and his child. Just as Lee Gordon does, Charles moves toward the assumption of responsibility for his own actions and his own fate. No longer will he rely upon his mother for support or use her smothering influence and his mingled affection for her as an excuse for his excesses. Instead of punishing himself and other women because of his oedipal urges and conflicts in attempting to hurt his mother, he will leave the very concept of punishment behind. It is impossible for Charles, black, alone, out of money, the future uncertain, to believe in freedom; but for the first time in his life he senses what the word means.

Despite its strongly confessional quality, *The Third Generation* succeeds as a novel, but there are some obvious problems with it. The overbearing reference to Charles's unresolved complex is one of them. "Through tying his story to a Freudian mother complex formula, ruthlessly applied," Riley Hughes wrote in his review of the book, "Mr. Himes removes his characters as far from the reader's sympathy as they are from convincing reality."[14] Hughes is not right concerning Himes's realism, but it is sometimes diffi cult to sympathize with Charles once the oedipal pattern has been established. It is difficult to understand why Charles, as intelligent as he is made out to be, does not recognize his problem earlier. Another diffi culty is the organization of the novel. Much tragic power is generated through the richly detailed case

study Himes presents, but, as Edmund Fuller showed,
the structural plan and the conception are not as good
as the writing skill with which the novel is carried
out.[15] The novel contains much beautiful description
and many powerful passages, but the only plan is
linear—we are introduced to Charles as a boy of three
and his story is simply carried straightforward from
there, although the traumatic scenes do afford a step-
by-step progression of anxiety moving toward the
moment of release. A third problem is simply a lack of
control in the ever-present force of anger and fear; the
problems of Charles Taylor are perhaps too apparent
to sustain the kind of controlled narrative that we find
in Himes's three earlier novels.

But *The Third Generation* nonetheless received
reviews that indicated growing interest in Himes and a
change in the attitudes that made the reception of
Lonely Crusade such a negative one. John Brooks,
for instance, remarked in the *New York Times* that
"Himes seems to have set out to grip the reader in a
vise of despair by cumulative incident and detail. His
searing book, with its terrible pathos of the oppressed
set against each other, shows how increasingly firm a
position he deserves among American novelists. But
the impact is weakened by the introduction, in several
cases, of chance misfortune unrelated to the characters
or their ancestry, and the whole seems at times to lack
a certain necessary measure of animal fun and human
hope."[16] There is not much animal fun in any of
Himes's earlier work, to be certain, and as traumatic a
series of events as *The Third Generation* recounts,
none should be expected. In Himes's next novel, however, despite a continuation of the confessional mode
and further development of the theme of self-destruction, Himes injects a considerable amount of humor,
wry and half-sad though it may be.

To mention humor at all in discussing a novel that ends with a drunken murder scene seems macabre, but *The Primitive*, while tragic in outline, is filled with incidents and conversations that are handled with ironic Rabelaisian gusto. Gargantuan drinking and eating scenes are described in a style that effectively blends the high and the low, and the literary allusion and street language are combined in a manner that makes *The Primitive*, despite its gruesomeness, more engaging than any of Himes's earlier novels. It is also a work in which Himes pushes to conclusion, in a psychologically satisfying way, two themes of frustration that had haunted him since *If He Hollers Let Him Go*: his anger at being rejected as a writer, and the black man's obsession with the white woman and what she represents. For Himes, *The Primitive* represents a stopping point, an end to his confessional phase, and a settling of scores.

The Primitive opens slowly with a series of contrasting chapters that alternately show Kriss Cummings, a white, middle-class woman executive, and Jesse Robinson, a black writer who does not know at first whether he is on the road to success or is down and out, moving through their separate lives and inevitably toward one another. As the novel continues, Himes effectively speeds up the back-and-forth movement, which is in itself a metaphor of the final sexual act that both Kriss and Jesse desire, until the reader, like the central characters themselves, goes through a blank-out and fears he has missed something. And then, horrifyingly, Himes reveals that the orgasmic moment not only had to happen, but that it did. And that is when Jesse, with the abruptness Himes so consistently uses, picks up the telephone to call the police.

The first chapter begins in Kriss's Gramercy Park apartment. She had slept with at least eighty-seven

men, had been married to a homosexual, and now at
thirty-seven-years-old awakens to fear and loneliness
each morning. Part of her morning routine, in addition
to taking a dexedrine and amylobarbitane pill to
straighten herself out, is to watch a talk show featuring a man named Glouscester and a chimpanzee,
apparently patterned on the old *Today* show featuring
Dave Garroway and J. Fred Muggs but with a difference—Glouscester's chimpanzee can predict the news
instead of simply comment on it. A sample: "Senator
Richard M. Nixon of California will be nominated for
Vice President, and on Sept. 28, 1952, he will go on
television . . . to defend a political fund placed at his
disposal by innocent and patriotic businessmen of California, most of whom have somehow become involved
in the real estate business and are hamstrung in their
desire to invest in low rental properties by the Demo-
cratic administrations rent-control program which,
paradoxically, precipitates high rent."[17] The chimpanzee returns again and again in the novel, most significantly in the last chapter, and symbolizes part of
what Himes means by the word primitive—that there
is an ape, a beast, in all of us, and that human behavior can be predicted on that basis. What better
Cassandra, then, but a chimpanzee?

The second chapter begins with Jesse waking up
in his Harlem room. As with the story of Bob Jones in
If He Hollers Let Him Go, Jesse's story begins with
dreams and his dream life provides a nightmarish
structure for his waking moments. He had been dreaming of falling through the ice while skating and none
of the couples skating nearby would pay any attention
to him, the dream apparently a metaphor of his present condition—about to go under and no one cares.
He is separated from his wife, he is running through
the $500 advance he received for the option on his

next novel, *I Was Looking for a Street*, and he needs a
drink. He gets up, has a water glass full of gin, and
goes back to sleep. He dreams again, this time of sitting at a banquet table between two empty chairs.
Then he walks down a flight of stairs to a parking lot
and watches a short, squat man beat a big, drunken
man with a chair. His being all alone at a banquet,
and his watching a beating both suggest Jesse's view
of his life in America—the inside world of plenty,
where he is not exactly rejected but not exactly welcome either, and the outside world of violence where
he is too often an unwilling spectator. He has a third
dream of being seventeen and kissing a beautiful girl
for the first time. He awakens from this dream of his
past and the sensation lingers.

His writer's mind tries to analyze the experience,
just as it has tried to deal with all of his past in his
books, trying to find the right word to describe the
experience. Part of his brain "was always tense, hyper-
sensitive, uncertain, probing—*there must be some
goddamned reason for this, for that. It had started
with the publication of his second book, five years
before. . . . Some goddamned reason for all the hate,
the animosity, the gratuitous ill will*—for all the pro-
cessed American idiocy, ripened artificially like canned
cheese."[18] Jesse is trying to find the answer as he is
trying to find the right word to describe his experience. And the word he finds, the word he defines with
the climactic act of his life, is the word *primitive*.

This process of definition is suggested by his repeated posing before mirrors and his later dream of
being lost in a house of mirrors. On this, the first morning of the story, he looks at his body in the mirror and
sees a lean figure, but his face, swollen with liquor,
shows his age. He turns away and drinks a breakfast
mixture of two raw eggs, milk and gin. He follows up

with several belts of whiskey and walks out into the
April sunshine. The bars are not open yet, so he starts
toward Forty-second Street to see what is showing at
the cheap theaters between Eighth Avenue and Times
Square.

The contrasting pattern continues in chapters
three and four. Kriss goes to her job at the India Institute on Madison Avenue where she is an assistant
director and makes $6,000 a year. Her job consists
mainly of writing summaries of institute projects to be
sent to subsidizing foundations and the U. S. State
Department. Jesse, meanwhile, has come up out of the
subway on the north side of Forty-second Street. He
looks in a bookstore for his own books but cannot find
them. He thinks of the many complaints about his
work he has received from editors; he thinks vaguely
of looking for a prostitute. He goes into a movie house
and there he gets the idea of calling Kriss, whom he
had met when she was working for a Chicago foundation that awarded grants to young writers. He picks up
a bottle of gin, goes to his room, waits until 6:30, and
calls and asks her out to dinner. She is busy, but she
will be free two nights later, on Thursday, and the
date is made.

Jesse shows up at Kriss's apartment already loos-
ened up on a few gin-and-beers. Neither appears to
the other as each had remembered. She had become a
handsome woman, but the daredevil girl was gone. As
for Jesse: "This man before her, in the old trench coat
she recognized immediately, was dead; hurt had settled so deep inside of him it had become part of his
metabolism."[19] They make small talk, but both are
aware of their mutual loneliness, of the passing of ex-
citement from their lives. At dinner he is distracted by
reflections of himself, by thoughts of the last time he
had seen her when he had gotten drunk and insulting

at a party during the manic summer after he had been
at a writers' and artists' colony. He thinks of other
drunken parties, of people they had known in Green-
wich Village. After finishing their steaks, Jesse and
Kriss return to Kriss's apartment where she makes him
swear he is telling the truth about being through with
his wife. Like Jackie Forks in *The Lonely Crusade*, the
most demeaning thing Kriss thinks she could do as a
white woman is to fight with a black woman over a
black man. Jesse and Kriss start drinking hard and
fast, and both of them pass out—and from this point
on, the novel moves from one blank-out to another.

When Jesse comes to, he pours the rest of the
Scotch and bourbon in a water glass and drinks it. His
prescription for the world, as he says to himself, is
continuous drunkenness. And his drinking is wildly
Rabelaisian. He consumes huge quantities, and his wit
is fired by the alcohol. But at the same time Jesse is, as
he admits himself, the kind of man who "could never
let a good glow be."[20] His constant anxiety, an anxiety
induced by the racial tension with which he has had to
live both in his life and in his art, never allows him to
let the world seem bright for long. So he drinks a glass
of vermouth and takes on a bitter edge as he and Kriss
sit at the breakfast table watching Glouscester and the
chimp, who predicts American charges of slave labor
in Russia and ends with a prophecy of police firing on
black rioters in Kimberly, South Africa. Again the pre-
dictions are of human acts that occur through in-
human motivation. Jesse makes a date for Saturday
and goes home, making certain no one sees him leaving a white woman's apartment at that time of day.

He is hit by nauseating depression when he gets
back to his room. "Jesse Robinson," he says to himself,
"There must be some simple thing in this life you don't
know. Some little thing. Something every other person

knows but you."[21] But one thing he does know is that there is no escape for someone who refuses to seek accommodation with white society—no matter how much he drinks. He thinks of the time he was thrown in jail in Bridgeport for a traffic accident that clearly was not his fault, and he wonders why he should be so upset about it still; after all, it happens every day. He thinks on—about his separation from his wife, about his own false sense of nobility, and about how other writers always seem to miss expressing what he sees and feels. He goes out to buy a bottle.

Kriss meanwhile waits for Dave, one of her lovers, who had borrowed $75 from her. When he arrives, she alternately antagonizes and entices him. After he is gone, she throws a handful of sleeping pills into her mouth, thinking she is committing suicide, but only four go down. She passes out on her bed.

When the narrative shifts back to Jesse, we learn that he has received a note instructing him to stop in at his publisher's office. His editor, James Pope, tells him that the publisher has decided to drop the option on Jesse's new novel, *I Was Looking for a Street*, claiming that the public is tired of protest novels and that Jesse's book lacks the necessary humor. (There is an echo here of much of the critical reaction to *The Third Generation*.) Jesse tries to argue, mentioning Rabelais in defense of passages that are considered too vulgar and *Hamlet* in response to the charge of excessive violence, but he soon realizes that to protest is useless. The editor suggests that he write a success novel, a story about blacks that would be inspirational. Jesse picks up his manuscript, which has been nicely wrapped for him, and leaves.

Back in his room he counts his money and sees that he has less than $200 of the $500 advance left. He drinks some bourbon and blanks out. He finds himself an hour later talking to a black man and a woman in a restaurant about solving the "Negro problem" through an all-black state or through black capitalism. He goes to a bar and starts drinking gin and beer. He wakes up in a theater watching a gangster film, then he is conscious of walking on a sidewalk with a woman on his arm, remembering suddenly that he had bought her drinks at Small's bar for an hour. His odyssey ends as he enters his room. He does not know what has happened to the woman. He pulls a copy of Gorky's *Bystander* off the shelf and reads the same two lines over and over, convinced they hold a secret message: "But was there really a boy? Perhaps there was no boy at all!" The lines suggest the doubts Jesse has about his own existence, and he once again starts running word combinations through his mind, hoping to hit on a solution of some kind: "problem-woman . . . problem-Negro . . . problem-white . . . white-woman . . . end-boy. . . . end-problem . . . end-white . . . end-end. . . ."[22] The combinations do not seem to work, but they do indicate where Jesse is heading—toward the end of something and that ending involves the end-end of the Negro-white, white woman-black boy problem as far as he is concerned.

This ending is foreshadowed and justified in the dream Jesse has after he again passes out. He sees himself in a house of mirrors where all the reflections are grotesque. He runs outside in terror and there he sees people of all races working side by side with normal expressions on their faces and thinking normal thoughts, "but from his point of view this normal struggle for existence appeared so greatly distorted by emotional idiocy, senseless loves and hatred, lunatic ambitions, bestial passions, grotesque reasoning, fantastic behavior, that he turned in horror and fled back into the house of distorted mirrors where by comparison everything seemed normal."[23] His drunkard's vision, fueled by his racial frustrations, distorted though it may be, is far less distorted than the outlook of those who go about their business assuming that love and harmony can be a social reality. At nine the next morning, he takes out his clasp knife and stabs his manuscript. That afternoon he is sitting in a bar and he sees a woman looking at his reflection. "You see that guy," he says. "That's what the white folks call a primitive. Don't let that worry you, baby. They like primitives. He's dangerous, a menace to society. He'd just as soon be white, rich, and respected as black, poor, and neglected. Proves right there he's crazy."[24]

That evening Jesse shows up at Kriss's apartment with two kinds of steak, a pound of veal kidneys, pork sausage, Scotch, bourbon, gin, and vermouth, and they begin a gargantuan drinking, eating, and arguing binge that brings the novel to a denouement that is at once brilliant and numb, like the perceptions of an alcoholic who is losing all control and knows it.

Their drinking starts with the Scotch and an argument about the past. She wants to know why he did not marry her as he had promised and if he is still seeing his wife. They watch Sid Caesar and Imogene Coca until one of Kriss's old lovers, Harold, arrives. The three of them talk drunkenly about Jesse's last book, which Harold was going to review but somehow did not. Harold starts crying and puts his head in Kriss's lap. Jesse pulls him up and insists that he leave; instead, Kriss goes into the bedroom and locks the door. Jesse and Harold eat a supper of half-burned, half-raw steak alone. Kriss emerges, another argument starts before Harold finally goes, and the next thing Jesse knows is that it is Sunday afternoon.

Kriss gets up first and has breakfast. Jesse is dreaming on the couch of millions of blacks being pushed off a cliff by laughing whites on horses. He falls onto the floor and wakes up to see Kriss grinning at him. He cleans up, makes himself a bourbon highball, and has sausage and kidneys for breakfast. Afterwards he and Kriss sit very civilly and watch Zoo Parade. Don, a homosexual friend of Kriss's, calls and says he will be over. Don had been jailed on a morals charge his senior year at Harvard and then, thanks to family money, had set himself up on Riverside Drive as a patron of blacks. Don starts to talk about his affair with a black army officer and Jesse tries to make it to the bathroom, but passes out. It is after seven when he comes to in bed.

When he gets up, Kriss is watching her favorite television program, Mr. Peepers. Jesse looks at himself again in the mirror and wonders what he expects to see. He turns to look at Kriss and is even more repelled—he has to laugh at himself, a black man repelled by a white woman. He drinks half a glass of gin. "For her," Himes writes, "this was the best part of it, all her past hurts were dissolved, watching the symptomatic self-destruction of a frustrated Negro male in a white woman's room."[25] He attacks her, pushing her down on the floor, but the telephone interrupts him. Walter Martin, the editor of a Negro picture magazine, and his wife Lucille are coming over. Walter is the sort who has his hair straightened every two weeks. Walter starts talking about the problem of slums in San Francisco, then shifts to a discussion of the limited audience for Jesse's books. Jesse gets drunker and makes fun of Walter, referring to him as boss. Jesse finally loses his temper, grabs a kitchen knife, and chops the head off a whiskey bottle. Walter tells him that he has got to join the human race; Jesse says that he has been an ape too long to change. The argument ends with Walter pulling a

switchblade knife and his wife restraining him. After
Walter and Lucille go home, Jesse hits Kriss with his
fist and knocks her down. She struggles to her feet,
defiantly takes off her clothes, and goes into the bedroom. Jesse drinks a slug of sherry and passes out.

He dreams of writing an account of himself as a
cook on a country estate. The book is called *Paradise
for Pigs* and describes a farm where hogs were able to
make sausage without being slaughtered. Then one
day a pig refuses to give sausage and is taken to the
slaughterhouse, the other pigs squealing *traitor* at him.
The rebel pig is, of course, like the heroes of Jesse's
novels and like Jesse himself—refusing to give of himself more than he wants to, refusing to write the uplift
novel, refusing to leave the house of distorted mirrors
to live in the fool's paradise outside.

Jesse wakes up on the couch with no idea of what
time it is. Again he stops to look in the mirror at his
embalmed visage and then goes into Kriss's room,
where she appears to be sleeping. He sees that it is
8:23 in the morning. He drinks some vermouth and
takes a shower, then once more turns on the television
set to Glouscester and the chimp. He hears another
prediction of the news, but this time it is a prediction
of the outcome of his own trial for murdering Kriss
with a knife. He shakes his head, thinking he has been
reading too much Faulkner. The chimp continues with
the news that Jesse will be electrocuted in Sing Sing
on 9 December. The peculiar thing about the case, the
chimp notes, is that there is no evidence of rape. And
then he goes on to predict that the Supreme Court will
outlaw racial segregation on 17 May 1954.

Kriss's maid arrives, and Jesse cannot believe
what he has just heard. He goes into Kriss's bedroom,
and crawls into bed. He dreams of running across end-
less glaciers, then he awakens to find that Kriss's body

is cold to his touch. His first impulse is to deny that he
had intended to kill her, but he knows that from the
first time he was hurt for being black that he would
eventually do what he has done. "End product of the
impact of Americanism on one Jesse Robinson—black
man," Jesse concludes. "Your answer, son. You've been
searching for it. *Black man kills white woman.* All the
proof you need now. Absolutely incontrovertible be-
haviorism of a male human being. Most human of all
behavior. Human beings only species of animal life
where males are known to kill their females. Proof
beyond all doubt. Jesse Robinson joins the human
race."[26] His act was a rejection of his conscience, the
conscience he had possessed when he was a primitive.
As he says to himself, "Your trouble, son, you tried too
hard to please. Not restricted by conscience like a
primitive. Reason why he's human. All other animals
restricted by conscience. Call it instinct but conscience
just the same. Reason why your own life was so bitter,
son. Had conscience."[27] Is integration practical? Will
it work? Are blacks actually equal? Jesse Robinson
provides the ironic answer.

Himes thus turns around one of the dominant
themes not only in Rabelais but also in American
culture—the notion that man is perfectible, or at least
the idea that a healthy, wise, gallant, and happy type
of man is possible and that there is such a thing as a
just society. The solution to the "Negro problem" had
long been seen in terms of bringing a primitive people
step-by-step toward equality, and the Supreme Court
decision was looked to as the culmination of this process. But equality implies being *equal to* something,
and that something is the white American. But for
Himes, this is a negative process because it is a step
not toward perfectibility but against it in his vision of
America as not a melting pot but an "Alchemy Com-

pany," into which Jesse Robinson went as "a primitive,
filled with things called principles, integrity, honor,
conscience, faith, love, hope, charity and such, and
came out the front door a human being, completely
purged."[28]

A purgation of another sort is dealt with in the
novel as far as Himes himself is concerned. His rejection as a writer and his outrage at it is effectively
represented in the figure of Jesse who, though turned
down by his publisher and enormously depressed because of his failure to find an audience, nonetheless
does find what the good writer is ultimately after—the
right words to describe himself and his condition. And
in the destruction of Kriss, Himes symbolically eliminates the specter of the white woman that had
haunted the heroes of his novels since Bob Jones's first
encounter with Madge in *If He Hollers Let Him Go*.
As Edward Margolies points out, the black man's at-
traction to the white woman is a major theme in
Himes. On one level the white woman is associated
with fear because interracial sex connotes death and
castration. But because of the mysterious taboo that is
also associated with her, the white woman is often
seen as irresistible. But the desire for her is mingled
with hatred and repulsion as far as black men are
concerned "since she is viewed as the original cause of
their pariah status; moreover, possessing a white
woman may serve as an act of clandestine revenge on
the white man who persecutes them."[29]

But killing a white woman is another matter, especially if she is killed as Kriss is, not out of fear, not
as the aftermath of rape, but as Othello kills Des-
demona, out of anger and jealousy, out of distinctly
human, not simply racial, urges. Himes has thus
moved to the resolution of a theme that is far different
from the blundering murder scene of Bigger Thomas

in *Native Son*. For Jesse, murdering Kriss is an act not directed against white society, but against himself. She has become a part of himself that he does not like. And Himes depicts, for perhaps the first time in a novel by a black American writer, a crime committed by a black man against a white woman that is, once Jesse realizes what he has become, more human than racial in its implications. The irony is, of course, that this is not necessarily better.

With *The Primitive*, Himes does, however, bring a phase of his writing to a close. It is the last of his confessional novels and ends the autobiographical emphasis that occasionally interferes with the structure of his work. The novel was finished in Europe and coincides with Himes's rejection of the United States and his desire for a different kind of life in a different culture free from American "alchemy" and the pressures that drove Jesse Robinson to destroy himself in the process of becoming "equal." As Himes later wrote, "All the while I was writing *The End of a Primitive* (the original title), this thought was uppermost in my mind: 'I'll give them something to hate me for; I'll give them this book, because this is the kind of thing they can really hate me for.' "[30] But the giving of hatred also was a working-out of hatred, and the ending of *The Primitive* is, in its way, as positive a conclusion as that of *Lonely Crusade*, only it is not an optimistic one. It does, however, point to a new development. When Jesse asks to speak to homicide, he thinks, "Good thing I read detective stories, wouldn't know what to do otherwise."[31]

Search Warrants
for the Inner City

"Down these mean streets a man must go who is not himself mean. . . ."

—*Raymond Chandler*, "The Simple Act of Murder"

Himes's sudden turn to the detective story in the mid-
1950s at first dismayed (and to a certain extent still
does dismay) many of his readers who had become
accustomed to the kind of confessional indictments he
had written from *If He Hollers Let Him Go* down to
The Primitive. The detective novels, beginning with
For Love of Imabelle in 1957, seemed to be potboilers,
attempts by a jaded, down-and-out expatriate who
had never made much money from his "legitimate"
novels to capitalize on a sensationalized and not always so accurately remembered depiction of a Harlem
entirely in the grip of criminals. But as Himes continued to write his Coffin Ed Johnson and Grave Digger Jones series, it became apparent that Himes had
not only developed a new form of the detective story,
but that he had found a means of expressing his vision
of a racially obsessed and decadent America that none
of his earlier books quite afforded. Recognition of
Himes's achievement was slow to develop, but by the
time *Blind Man with a Pistol* came out in 1969, hesita-
tions concerning Himes's artistic integrity had been

exchanged for such critical enthusiasms as this one: "Of all the black American writers now working the vein of imagination, Chester Himes alone seems to have carved out for himself an area of confrontation that is applicable—and meaningful—effective social protest and effective art."[1] The effectiveness of Himes's protest and his art in his detective novels derives from the interplay of character and setting; that is, his powerful conception of his two black detectives and their role as Virgilian guides to an inner city that is at once Harlem, hell, and the nightmare center of white America.

The success of a detective story seems, upon first consideration, to be a matter of plot—arranging incidents so that the reader is under a compulsion to find out who did it (and the *it* is usually a murder). But a far greater matter in the genre is characterization, particularly the ability to develop a memorable central character, the detective. From Carroll John Daly's Race Williams in the early *Black Mask* magazine stories of the 1920s through Dashiell Hammett's Sam Spade of *The Maltese Falcon*, Raymond Chandler's Philip Marlowe of *The Big Sleep*, Mickey Spillane's Mike Hammer, and Ross Macdonald's Lew Archer, the personality of the detective hero has been the major factor in making memorable the novels in which they appear. All of these heroes, and to a certain extent Coffin Ed and Grave Digger, are in the mold of the original *Black Mask* hard-boiled detective.

Black Mask, the pulp magazine started by H. L. Mencken and George Jean Nathan in the spring of 1920 (they sold it for a considerable profit just six months later), specialized in tautly told and even more tautly written stories of objective realism. Captain Joseph T. Shaw, who took over editorship of the magazine in November 1926, encouraged the development of a new type of detective story not based on the principle of ratiocination—the conception of the crime story as a puzzle to be solved by a detective who is essentially a man of thought, not action—that had been characteristic of the tales of Poe and Arthur Conan Doyle. The kind of detective Shaw had in mind often is forced to act before he thinks, because the world with which the detective must deal is a violent one that is better dealt with through involvement than through retreat to the study with a smoking jacket and pipe, like Sherlock Holmes. As Philip Durham writes, the *Black Mask* "heroes were violent, but their violence was not merely that of sensationalism. It was rather a kind of meaningful violence, sometimes symbolic of a special ethical code or attitude, sometimes an explicit description and implicit criticism of a corrupt society."[2] A good example of this type of hero is Hammett's Continental Op, a nameless fat man working for the Continental Detective Agency, who in two long stories in *Black Mask*, "The Big Knock-Over" and "106,000 Blood Money," solves a huge bank robbery, carried out by one hundred and fifty of the country's most skillful gangsters, by arranging to have the hoods eliminate each other until the field is sufficiently narrowed so that the Op can recover the money. Fourteen of the criminals are killed, then six more, and the death toll mounts so rapidly that the St. Valentine's Day Massacre seems like a misdemeanor. The Op is on the side of right, but he is in many ways as cruel and as unscrupulous in pursuing his cause as his opponents are in pursuing theirs. He is a deadly shot with a pistol, able to give and take vicious beatings with his fists, and he foreshadows Coffin Ed and Grave Digger in these respects.

But Himes's detectives are black; they must operate in the Harlem of the 1950s and 1960s; and they never are allowed to deal with such classically simple crimes as a gangland bank robbery. Their personalities, the situations they find themselves in, and the philosophical implications of their actions are far more complicated than those of the Continental Op or those of any other hard-boiled heroes. Chandler's Philip Marlowe, however, has some affinity with Coffin Ed and Grave Digger, not only because the Los Angeles in which he works is developed symbolically somewhat like Himes's Harlem, but because he is an urban hero who is appalled by the corruption of the modern city and, in defiance of all reason, in a choice that is absurd, decides to take on search after search for the truth that solves the crime even though the solution often neither explains nor settles anything. "For the Continental Op, his work is no more than a job; but for Marlowe, his work is a defense of people and values," writes Herbert Ruhm in his study of Chandler.[3] Much the same is true of Coffin Ed and Grave Digger, and like Marlowe they move through a milieu that contains an incredible gradation of speech and class but is nonetheless a jungle, a wilderness of neon where the epitome of honor sometimes seems represented only by the conscience of a stool pigeon.

"As far back as Lieutenant Anderson could remember," Himes writes in *Cotton Comes to Harlem*, "both of them, his two ace detectives with their identical big hard-shooting, head-whipping pistols, had always looked like two hog farmers on a weekend in the Big Town."[1] Their nicknames indicate the respect they receive in Harlem, whose residents know that Grave Digger and Coffin Ed each has an invisible line over which no one had better step. They drive the streets in a nondescript battered Plymouth with a hopped-up engine. They work mainly through sheer presence and chance along with a carefully maintained network of stool pigeons—junkies, blind men who can see when the moment is right, drunks who sober up fast—who appear whenever they see the black Plymouth pull to a stop in their neighborhoods. And they must deal with a part of the city in which the daily police reports include such events as a man killing his wife with an ax because she burned a pork chop, a man playing a fatal game of Russian roulette in a bar with a .32-caliber revolver, and a man picked up with a shotgun and a hound dog for hunting cats on Seventh Avenue.

Both detectives are coldly efficient, so coldly efficient that the police commissioner has to call them on the carpet repeatedly for excessive violence, or, to use the term, police brutality. Most of this violence is directed at other blacks and this, as many reviewers have noted, seems paradoxical given the social consciences of the two detectives who never become hardened enough to cease shaking their heads over the wholesale victimization of their race. But Coffin Ed and Grave Digger see no other way to control crime than through brute force—unless social change takes place, and that is not likely. As Grave Digger says to his boss, "We got the highest crime rate on earth among the colored people in Harlem. And there ain't but three things to do about it: Make the criminals pay for it—you don't want to do that; pay the people enough to live decently—you ain't going to do that; so all that's left is let 'em eat one another up."[5] And the type of crime that outrages the two detectives most is the kind that occurs in *Cotton Comes to Harlem*—a hypocritical preacher extracting $87,000 from people gullible enough to sign up for his fake back-to-Africa movement. Coffin Ed and Grave Digger are more interested in recovering the money than in apprehending all of the criminals involved in the bizarre series of transactions concerning a bale of cotton in which the

money has been stashed, and in the end they make a
deal that does not even involve the original money, a
deal that allows one of the crooks to escape.

Himes's detectives often blend together as they go
into action, but they are contrasting types. Grave Digger has a lumpy face, reddish brown eyes that always
seem to smolder, a big and rugged frame, a battered
felt hat perched summer and winter on the back of his
head, and a black alpaca suit. He is more articulate
than Coffin Ed, who lets him ask most of the questions
when interrogating witnesses and suspects. Coffin Ed
has one distinct feature—his face, which has been
badly scarred by a glass of acid thrown at him by a
hoodlum. His appearance is so grotesque that he has
picked up another nickname, Frankenstein, and there
is more than a little resemblance to a monster in some
of Coffin Ed's behavior when angered. More than once
Grave Digger has to restrain him from strangling a
suspect or force him to lower his pistol. The two detectives live near one another with their wives and children in Astoria, Long Island, thirty-five minutes from
Harlem, and they both pack identical long-barreled,
nickel-plated .38-caliber revolvers on .44 frames, but
they are each representative of different impulses.
Grave Digger is hardly pure reason and Coffin Ed
does not embody mindless action, but the name Ed is
close enough to Freud's *Id* to indicate the essential
dichotomy between the two characters. In a sense they
are doubles, as Dr. Jekyll and Mr. Hyde or Poe's
Dupin and Minister D are doubles; but there are so
many instances in which the distinctions between reason and rage, between calculated reaction and the
instantaneous aiming and firing of a pistol, simply
cannot be maintained that it is a tossup between who
is in control and who ought to be in control—Grave
Digger who philosophizes and has visionary dreams or

Coffin Ed who has a reputation for being quick on the trigger. Either way, they get the job done.

Since finding out how they do it is one of the major appeals of the series in which they appear, rehearsing the plots of all the Grave Digger and Coffin Ed stories would, to a certain extent, ruin them as reading experiences. But two of the novels, *The Crazy Kill* and *Blind Man with a Pistol*, may be looked at in detail, both to give some idea of Himes's type of detective novel and to indicate how the form developed as he pursued it over the course of a decade.

Like all of the early Grave Digger and Coffin Ed stories, *The Crazy Kill*, published in the United States in 1959, begins with a bizarre crime and progresses through images of chaos and an astounding gallery of low-life characters toward a resolution that does not materialize until the last few pages. Outside the apartment where a wake is going on for the notorious gambler, Big Joe Pullen, a bag of money belonging to the manager of the A&P grocery across the street is stolen by a young thief. Reverend Short, Mamie Pullen's minister, a storefront preacher addicted to a mixture of opium and brandy, is leaning out of a bedroom window in Big Joe's flat watching the bag of money being lifted. He leans too far in his fascination and falls out. He lands in a basket of bread outside the bakery beneath, picks himself up, and staggers inside. Back at the wake, he says he sees a terrible vision—a dead man stabbed in the heart. Mamie accompanies Reverend Short to the window, looks down, and there she sees a body in the breadbasket, the body of Valentine Haines, a punk who was living with his sister Dulcy and her husband gambler Johnny "Fishtail" (for the fins on his big Cadillac) Perry. The question: Who murdered Val? It is up to Grave Digger and Coffin Ed to find out.

They begin by taking Johnny and Dulcy Perry, Mamie Pullen, Reverend Short, and yet another gambler, Chink Charlie, in for questioning, which is conducted in a room known to the Harlem underworld as the Pigeon Nest, a soundproof, windowless chamber with a three-hundred-watt spotlight focused on a wooden stool. Detective Sgt. Brody, a white Irishman, and the two black detectives do the questioning. None of those questioned knows anything and no one can identify the unusual stag-handle knife used in the killing. As Brody says, after two hours and seventeen minutes of this, "The coroner's report says the victim was killed where he lay. But nobody saw him arrive. Nobody remembers exactly when Chink Charlie left the flat. Nobody knows when Dulcy Perry left. Nobody knows for certain whether Reverend Short even fell out of the God-damned window."[6] Brody, despite his experience, cannot quite believe the incredible complications in the crime and has no idea of how or why such a murder was committed. Grave Digger tells him, in a line that echoes through the whole book and through the entire series, "This is Harlem, where anything can happen."[7]

Brody continues to do most of the questioning, but it is clear that as a white man he will get no answers. It is not simply that he does not know how to ask the right questions and ask them in the right way; it is because he is on alien ground. He is not as streetwise as Grave Digger and Coffin Ed; but then how could he be? The Harlem in which they have moved and operated for years is so distant from Brody's experience because he is white that he might as well be a creature from another planet. Brody is in a way an emblem of all white institutions; he is well-meaning even though despised by the people in his precinct, and he wants to understand black people. But there is

no way he can, no more than he can, like the Lieutenant Anderson of other novels, stop himself from making unconscious and unintentional racial slurs in the
presence of Grave Digger and Coffin Ed. Brody is, in
street language, the Man, but the two detectives are
the men, the ones who must descend into the inferno
to discover the truth. So back onto the mean streets
they go. Perhaps the culprit is Johnny, who is notorious for his bad temper and who might have gotten
tired of having Val hanging around. Perhaps it was
Chink Charlie, whose girl friend Doll Baby seemed
more than a little familiar with Val at times. But why
the breadbasket? Why the strange knife? And how
does the obviously deranged Reverend Short fit into all
of this?

The mystery unwinds through a string of memorable scenes—Fats's Down Home Restaurant (special
of the day—alligator tail and rice), Reverend Short
preaching Big Joe's funeral at the church of the Holy
Rollers, and Grave Digger and Coffin Ed cruising
down Seventh Avenue: "A numbers writer standing in
front of Madame Sweetiepie's hairdressing parlor,
flashing a handful of paper slips with the day's winning numbers, looked up and saw Coffin Ed's baleful
eyes pinned on him and began eating the paper slips
as though they were taffy candy."[8]

The two detectives begin by locating a potential
witness—the thief who stole the money from the
owner of the A&P. How do they find the thief? They
ask Gigolo, a heroin addict who is one of their stool
pigeons, if he has seen anyone around the pool halls
who seems to be luxuriating in new-found and unex-
plainable cash. They find their man, who puts them on
a trail that leads back to Reverend Short. The Reverend explains that on Big Joe Pullen's last trip to
Chicago, the gambler had learned that Val and Dulcy

were not brother and sister but that they, in fact, were husband and wife and still were, even though Johnny Perry thought he was married to Dulcy. Big Joe intended to tell Val to disappear; but Big Joe had died before he could get around to it. He did manage to tell Mamie about it, however, and she had come to the Reverend for spiritual advice on the matter. He said he would handle it. Reverend Short called Val over to the church the night of the wake and told him to leave within twenty-four hours or he would tell Johnny, who, if he knew the truth, might very well kill both Val and Dulcy. Later, while at the wake, Reverend Short felt compelled by God to go into Big Joe's bedroom and look through Big Joe's things. There he found the stag-handle knife, went to the window with it, and fell out. Meanwhile, Johnny and Val had driven up, seen the breadbasket, and decided to play a joke on the people at the wake. Val was to lie down in the breadbasket and Johnny would go to a telephone, call the Pullen's number, and tell the person who answers to look out the window at the dead man. Reverend Short was standing in the hallway out of sight trying to recover from the shock of his fall when he saw Val cross the street. As the Reverend explains, God instructed him to kill Val and he did, right then. There are several plot fragments and dead ends before all of this is revealed, among them Johnny's shooting of Chink Charlie (fatally) whom he finds naked in his apartment and Reverend Short's stabbing (not fatally) of Dulcy.

The murder turns out to be a "crazy" kill not only because the murderer is crazy but because it takes place for little apparent reason in a city where craziness is synonymous with coolness, and where there are apparently as many reasons why a man like Valentine Haines should be killed as that he not be killed. And what difference should it make that he has been murdered? The only ones who seem much concerned are Grave Digger and Coffin Ed who are placed in an absurd situation from the very beginning: black men trying to enforce the justice of a system that they themselves believe to be unjust to other black men. And when they catch the murderer, what do they have? A brandy-and-opium crazed preacher who may or may not have been aware that he was committing a crime.

Like *The Big Gold Dream* (1960) and the other early Grave Digger and Coffin Ed stories, *The Crazy Kill*, despite its existential overtones, is essentially a "mayhem" novel. That is, it carries the reader forward not simply through the step-by-step efforts of the detectives to solve the crime (indeed Grave Digger and Coffin Ed's progress could hardly be called step-by-step), but through a series of wild encounters in which pistols are drawn, fists thrown, the black Plymouth roars through the streets, and violence dominates.

But with *Cotton Comes to Harlem* (1965) and especially with *Blind Man with a Pistol* (1969) the tone changes. The violence remains, Grave Digger and Coffin Ed operate in the same way, and the term mayhem still applies, but the artistry has been combined more effectively, certainly more intentionally, with social protest. As Shane Stevens has written about *Blind Man with a Pistol*, Himes considers the book "his most important work. I suspect this is because he has put into this novel . . . much of his feeling about what is happening here in America."[9] This concern about what is happening in America goes back to Himes's first novels and is present to a certain extent in all of his writing, but in *Blind Man with a Pistol* his concerns and his solutions take on new shapes in what is most certainly the best of his detective novels.

"A friend of mine, Phil Lomax, told me this story about a blind man with a pistol shooting at a man who had slapped him on a subway train and killing an innocent bystander peacefully reading his newspaper across the aisle and I thought," Himes writes in his preface to the novel, "damn right, sounds just like to day's news, riots in the ghettoes, war in Vietnam, masochistic doings in the Middle East. And then I thought of some of our loudmouthed leaders urging our vulnerable soul brothers on to getting themselves killed, and thought further that all unorganized violence is like a blind man with a pistol."[10] Himes thus sets up the thesis of his novel in a way that underscores his seriousness. This is no ordinary detective story and Grave Digger and Coffin Ed are to take on a function that involves far more than their earlier roles as agents of mayhem.

The novel begins with an opening chapter that, without exaggeration, is one of the strangest in American literature. An old, condemned, three-story brick house on 119th Street with a sign in the front window indicating FUNERALS PERFORMED attracted no attention even though people living in the area had seen many black nuns entering and leaving the building. The house attracted no attention, that is, until another sign appeared in the window, this one advertising for fertile women. Two white policemen stop to investigate. They enter the house from the rear and find a fat, cretinous black man stirring a huge pot of foul-smelling stew atop a brick firebox built on the rusted floor of a Volkswagen. When one of the policemen asks the cretinous man a question, he gets hit on the head with the stew ladle. The second cop knocks the old man down just as a hoard of black nuns and naked screaming children run into the room followed by a very old man dressed in a white gown. He turns out to be

Reverend Sam, who explains that he is not a monk but a Mormon, that the nuns are all his wives, the naked children are all his children, and that he is one hundred years old. He explains the sign in the window by saying that one of his wives has died and he must replace her to keep the number up to twelve. When reinforcements arrive from the Harlem precinct station, the children are having their lunch—the stew poured into three rows of troughs, from which the children, on hands and knees, feed like pigs. The household, the officers learn, is apparently supported by the wives walking the streets begging alms. All this is beyond belief to the policemen. And when they find three graves in the basement, each containing the remains of a female body, they take Reverend Sam in.

The opening chapter not only emphasizes Himes's recurring theme that anything can happen in Harlem; it also serves to emphasize what life in Harlem has become in the course of the twentieth century. Years of segregation, broken promises of equality, economic oppression, and cultural isolation have turned what was once regarded by whites as an exotic community of happy darkies into a place of nightmares where the residents, like Reverend Sam, have a logic all their own for explaining their behavior: "All right, all right, but why didn't his children wear clothes? Why, it was more comfortable without them, and clothes cost money. And eat at tables, like human beings, with knives and forks? Knives and forks cost money, and troughs were more expedient; surely, as white gentlemen and officers of the law, they should understand just what he meant."[11] Reverend Sam's bizarre behavior should not be so shocking to the white officers; it, like most of the seeming eccentricities of life in Harlem, is simply expedient, given the conditions. But as time goes on, the conditions get more and more difficult. Reverend Sam is willing to raise his children as pigs, but how long will the children be content with the troughs? The crumbling building, the cretin at the stewpot, the old man with his stewpot religion, the women walking the streets as virgin nuns by day and turning into baby machines at night, the horde of naked children—all this is a metaphor of Harlem, the inner city of American racial consciousness. And the solution is not to take Reverend Sam down to the station. What is the solution? *Blind Man with a Pistol* explores several—brotherhood, black power, Black Jesus movement, the Black Muslims, sexual integration, and simple law and order.

The scene shifts in the second chapter to the "Mecca of Harlem," where 125th Street crosses Seventh Avenue. This is the locale of the old Theresa Hotel where the world's greatest black celebrities have stayed. It is also a place through which many white people pass daily because of transit routes. It is, in a sense, a racial interface, a place where whites and blacks meet, but not always wisely, safely, or well, as a white, middle-aged homosexual finds out after meeting a young black male prostitute who is wearing a red fez in the Theresa building lunch counter at 2 A.M. on a hot summer morning. A few hours later, Grave Digger and Coffin Ed are driving slowly west on 123rd Street in the old Plymouth when they see a man in a red fez running ahead of them carrying a pair of light gray pants over one arm. They let him go; to them there is nothing unusual in a black man stealing the pants of a white man who is probably in bed with a whore. It happens all the time in Harlem and if white citizens want their kicks, they have to take the risks. But then a bare-legged white man staggers onto the sidewalk. The detectives jump out and grab him. The front of his shirt is covered with blood spurting from his jugu-

lar vein. Grave Digger tries to get the man to tell who
did it, but all he gets is a gurgle. They call into the
precinct station and Lieutenant Anderson tells them to
stay there until the experts, the homicide detectives
arrive. Residents of the neighborhood gather around,
but as usual no one knows anything. The blood trail
leads to an obscenely decorated pad next to the boiler
room in the basement of an apartment building. Lucas
Covey, the manager of the building, admits, after
being pistol-whipped and almost choked to death by
Coffin Ed, that he rented the pad to a man named
John Babson. Is this the name the dying man tried to
pronounce?

At the same time, another even more grisly incident is taking place. Doctor Mubuta, a fake African
witch doctor, who may or may not be the Reverend
Sam of the opening chapter, is about to administer a
youth elixir composed of albumen, baboon testicles,
and cyanide to an aged black racketeer who wants to
be rejuvenated so he can marry a white teenaged girl.
The racketeer has a gladstone bag full of money for
Doctor Mubuta, who claims to have the only solution
for "the Negro Problem." "We're gonna outlive the
white folks," he says. "While they has been concentrating on ways of death, I has been concentrating on how
to extend life. While they'll be dying, we'll be living
forever . . . will be alive to see the day when the black
man is the majority on this earth, and the white man
his slave."[12] But the old racketeer's present wife, who
is listening to all of this, rushes at the young white girl
with a switchblade. Knives flash all over the room. The
wife is stabbed. The racketeer's lawyer is stabbed in
the head. The racketeer's chauffeur is stabbed. And
Doctor Mubuta, just as he is about to run out the door
with the money, is stabbed by a short black man in a
red fez who is entering the apartment. The man in the
fez takes the gladstone bag and runs.

The man in the fez provides an ironic reply to Doctor Mubuta's theory of outliving the white folks, but he provides no answers for Grave Digger and Coffin Ed. What is the connection between the murder of the white homosexual and the theft of the gladstone bag? Grave Digger and Coffin Ed want to find out, but they are hindered by the precinct captain, who is on the verge of retirement and does not want to go out with the exposure of a scandal involving homosexual prostitution, racketeering, and who knows what else in his precinct. So Grave Digger and Coffin Ed are assigned to investigate the brush-fire riots that are taking place. The captain thinks an instigator is behind them.

What the Captain does not know is that three movements have been building toward confrontation in Harlem on Nat Turner Day. First, there is Marcus Mackenzie, who, along with his middle-aged Swedish mistress, has a vision of brotherhood—blacks and whites with their arms around one another marching toward peace, freedom, and equality. His gospel is based on a mixture of Christianity and interracial sex. Second, there is Black Power, masterminded by a mysterious Doctor Moore, whose black Cadillac limousine has a BLACK POWER sign that converts to a BROTHERHOOD sign depending upon what neighborhood he is in. Behind his double front, he is a pimp who sends his high-priced whores to work the cocktail parties at the Americana. What he wants is to make a mint off the looting that would follow a riot, but for that he needs a dead man, a black man killed by a white policeman. And third, there is The Temple of Black Jesus run by General Ham, a man with a harelip, who proposes that his followers march with the statue of the Black Jesus (Jesus in a grotesque pose, a rope around his neck, and a sign underneath, THEY LYNCHED ME) "until whitey pukes."[13] The three groups collide at Seventh Avenue and 125th Street as

Grave Digger and Coffin Ed watch, the two detectives powerless to even control the bands of juvenile delinquents that are following the marchers.

Grave Digger and Coffin Ed go back and tell Lieutenant Anderson that they know who is responsible—Abraham Lincoln for freeing the slaves without making provisions for feeding them. But then Lincoln cannot be convicted because he could plead good intentions, and no white man is convicted for that. Anderson complains about the way they are putting him on, so they say they know the real culprit. "Some call him lack of respect for law and order, some lack of opportunity, some the teachings of the Bible, some the sins of their father," Grave Digger says. "Some call him ignorance, some rebellion. Me and Ed look at him with compassion. We're victims."[14] Grave Digger tells Anderson that they are the victims of white skin—and that is what is making blacks run through the streets looting. "It's a question of law," Grave Digger adds; "if the law don't feed us, who is?"[15] For blacks, the law simply has not been enforced equitably and legally; it has been used as a means of oppression. Instead of helping, it hinders. Instead of providing nourishing conditions, it has been used to legalize starvation. That is why precinct captains never retire broke. If you want order, Coffin Ed emphasizes, you must enforce the law. Enforce it to protect the people, not the racketeers. Why do the people loot? Because they are being starved by the law instead of being nourished by it. Reverend Sam's children may look healthy, but that does not mean they like eating out of troughs.

The detectives make their point, but Lieutenant Anderson sends them out to check on the Black Muslims. Perhaps Michael X, the minister of the Harlem Mosque, can tell them who is behind the riots. For the sake of getting a statement to bring back to the captain, Grave Digger and Coffin Ed secure an interview with the minister. Michael X answers their question right off. The man behind it all is "Mister Big," but Michael X refuses to reveal Mister Big's identity other than to tell them to ask their boss, who knows. And Grave Digger and Coffin Ed are left without a statement to take to the station. They warn Michael X about talking the way he has—it is a good way to get killed, they tell him.

The central character in the next-to-last chapter is a blind man who does not want anyone to think he is blind. He walks the streets from memory, shoots dice by ear, and stumbles aboard a subway train. A discontented black gardener who is talking to himself in a loud voice about the miseries of his job and the way his white employer treats him thinks the blind man is staring at him. The two get into an argument fanned by the baiting of a burly white truck driver. A black clergyman in clerical collar tries to stop the dispute by preaching against violence. When the white man charges down the aisle and hits the blind man, the blind man pulls a revolver from underneath his coat and mistakenly shoots the preacher in the heart. The blind man continues to fire as the train comes to the 125th Street station.

When the final chapter opens, Grave Digger and Coffin Ed are standing in the street where Lenox Avenue crosses 125th Street shooting rats that are running from some condemned buildings being demolished by a wrecking ball. People in the neighborhood are embittered by the urban renewal project and are angrily watching the crane swing the steel ball into the crumbling tenements. Wisecrackers from the corner bar are enjoying seeing the two detectives blast away with the long-barrelled, nickel-plated .38-caliber pistols. On another corner, four white policemen are also observing the marksmanship of Grave Digger and Coffin Ed. Just then the gardener, followed moments later by the white truck driver, comes running up out of the subway entrance. When the blind man emerges and fires two shots in the direction of the truck driver, the white patrolmen cut him down, the cry goes out that an innocent soul brother has been killed by the white police and a major riot begins. When Grave Digger calls in and tells Anderson that a blind man with a pistol started it, the lieutenant says that it does not make any sense. Grave Digger agrees, and the novel ends.

As a detective story, the novel itself does not make sense in the way the genre demands. Grave Digger and Coffin Ed do not get their man; they never find out who the man in the red fez is. They are thwarted both by the system (the captain does not want them to find out something) and the consequences of the system having been unequally enforced for too long (the riots). The reader is left with an uneasy feeling because the loose ends of the story are not tied together—a feeling that effectively reinforces Himes's depiction of the social order coming unravelled. And looming over it all is the form of the blind man with his pistol.

The theme of blindness runs throughout the novel, beginning with the failure of the white patrolmen to notice anything unusual about Reverend Sam's old funeral home until he placed the fertile-women-wanted sign in the window. And even then the policemen cannot believe their eyes. The point is apparent: the agents of white America have been blind to what has actually been going on in Harlem for too many years. Implications of blindness also extend to Grave Digger and Coffin Ed. Partly because of the captain's interference, partly because of a lack of cooperation from the black people upon whom they must depend for information, and partly because of changing times, Grave Digger and Coffin Ed fail to discover who is behind the murders they are trying to investigate. It is the latter point, changing times, that most seems to obscure matters for the two detectives, and in this the differences between *Blind Man with a Pistol* and *The Crazy Kill* are apparent.

In *The Crazy Kill*, Grave Digger and Coffin Ed have to deal only with gamblers and a crazy preacher. Harlem is a place of incredible depravity and the detectives must constantly be ready to meet violence with violence. But the crime they are called upon to solve is, despite its bizarre nature, simply a classic murder involving the same murder weapon that has figured in so many other whodunits—an unusual knife. But in *Blind Man with a Pistol*, Grave Digger and Coffin Ed are working in a fog of social forces. Gamblers and opium-addict preachers are one thing to deal with; Brotherhood, Black Power, Black Jesus, and the Black Muslims are quite another matter. And instead of a single murder set up narratively in such a way that the careful reader guesses fairly early that Reverend Short is the culprit, there are multiple murders and the connecting link is a man in a red fez who may or may not be a Black Muslim and who may or may not be connected with the syndicate. The reader is not even certain whether or not the appearances of the man in the red fez actually involve the same character. The degree of chaos has increased so much in their inner city that Grave Digger and Coffin Ed are unable to do much more than preserve their own lives if not their dignity (in one scene, when a molotov cocktail is dropped on the roof of the Plymouth, Grave Digger's pants catch on fire and he winds up standing in the street in his purple shorts).

The chaos is compounded by the rhetoric of the revolutionary organizations that figure in the book. In his depiction of these groups, Himes expresses his revulsion at the simplistic slogans and ideas they use as solutions for the problems of black people in the United States.[16] Marcus Mackenzie of Brotherhood is propounding a solution that is simply too naïve, that the conflict between blacks and whites will cease if the two races get to know each other better. The Black Power advocates are described as storm troopers and the man behind the scenes, Doctor Moore, is patently dishonest. The Black Jesus movement is based on a defensible enough notion, that Christianity with its emphasis on forgiveness and love has been useful to whites in helping to keep blacks in line. But what good will it do to march with the lynched image of the Black Jesus? And it seems somewhat suspicious that General Ham is met outside the temple by a buxom white woman with blue-dyed hair driving a lavender Cadillac Coupe de Ville. The Black Muslims are treated more sympathetically. While waiting in the Black-Art bookstore for Michael X to appear, Grave Digger and Coffin Ed are led to a back room by the bookstore owner where the walls are hung with autographed pictures of internationally famous black people and the room itself is scattered with African headgear, shields, spears, masks, and ceremonial robes. "In that room," Himes writes, "it was easy to believe in a Black World, and black racism seemed more natural than atypical."[17] But that room is not the streets of Harlem, and when the bookstore owner lectures the two detectives on black history, showing them instruments that were used in the slave trade, Coffin Ed says that he knows he is descended from slaves. What is the bookstore owner trying to say? He tells them that they should be free now that the time is right. But Grave

Digger and Coffin Ed know that freedom is not that easy to come by. Michael X, when he appears, is described as young and vulnerable even though he makes his appearance with dignity. But he is "absurdly defiant,"[18] and his position, despite being presented much more compassionately by Himes than those of the other groups, involves a kind of willful blindness, a failure to see the larger picture as far as the problems of black people in America are concerned.

But just what is this larger picture toward which Himes points? It is not that Himes is against the objectives of the groups he attacks in *Blind Man with a Pistol*. And it is not that he is against the idea of riots to gain social objectives. It is that the groups and the riots that they precipitate are misdirected because of a kind of blindness that is a consequence both of the internalized culture of Harlem itself and the perverse willingness of human nature to accept simple answers to complex problems. Like the blind man with the pistol, the groups that clash on Nat Turner Day think they are aiming at the white man, but what they succeed in doing is to destroy each other. The violence that results is unorganized, and it leads nowhere, other than to set the mood for the subsequent riot when the blind man is killed at the subway entrance.

Grave Digger and Coffin Ed are, of course, organized violence. The viciousness with which they go after their men is viciousness based on the belief that the law must be enforced, that however crooked the world in which they must operate is, the two detectives must be honest and unswerving in their pursuit of justice. As Himes indicates, in their twelve years on the force, neither Grave Digger nor Coffin Ed has taken a bribe. They have had to take beatings from criminals and have been repeatedly thwarted and abused by their precinct captain and the commissioners. Now they are middle-aged, have been denied promotion, and their salaries have not kept up with the cost of living. But amid incredible corruption, they have retained their integrity even if their work seems as futile as standing on the street and shooting rats running from a condemned building.

But while Grave Digger and Coffin Ed are unable to see their way through to apprehending the man in the red fez, they are not blind to what is happening around them. They do not find the truth behind the murders as detectives are supposed to, but they come to understand a larger truth that is more important. This discovery comes out of their assignment to find out who is instigating the riots. The two detectives wonder about what makes the new generation in Harlem so much different from their own. What made the young blacks confront the white police one day and then write complex poetry and dream incredible dreams the next? It cannot all be blamed on slum conditions or broken homes. Coffin Ed asks Grave Digger to explain what has happened, and Grave Digger does:

Hell, Ed, you got to realize times have changed since we were sprites. These youngsters were born just after we got through fighting a war to wipe out racism and make the world safe for the four freedoms. And you and me were born just after our pappys had got through fighting a war to make the world safe for democracy. But the difference is that by the time we'd fought in a jim crow army to whip the Nazis and had come home to our native racism, we didn't believe any of that shit. We knew better. We had grown up in the Depression and fought under hypocrites against hypocrites and we'd learned by then that whitey is a liar. Maybe our parents were just like our children and believed their lies but we had learned the only difference between the home-grown racist and the foreign racist was who had the nigger. Our side won so our white rulers were able to keep their niggers so they would yap to their heart's content about how they were going to give us equality as soon as we were ready.[19]

This is a theme that appears in *If He Hollers Let Him Go* and is a more or less constant factor in Himes's novels. The difference, as Grave Digger emphasizes, is that what had saved his generation is that they had never believed that white America was going to give them equality. "But this new generation believes it. And that's how we get riots."[20] But this does not mean that Grave Digger and Coffin Ed believe that riots are going to lead anywhere. They are too street-hardened, too cynical for that. Times have changed, but the enforcement of justice has become more difficult than ever. Grave Digger and Coffin Ed see and understand what has happened, but the man in the red fez is still on the loose, Doctor Moore has his dead man, and Grave Digger and Coffin Ed are powerless. But the two detectives serve nonetheless as effective instruments of social criticism.

Ross Macdonald in "The Writer as Detective Hero" writes that "A close paternal or fraternal relationship between writer and detective is a marked peculiarity of the form. Throughout its history, from Poe to Chandler and beyond, the detective hero has represented his creator and carried his values into action in society."[21] If this is true, Grave Digger and Coffin Ed with their combination of toughness, honesty, and willingness to enforce justice through controlled violence are central to an understanding of Himes's ideas and Himes himself. And the development of the two detectives as they move from the relatively understandable setting of *The Crazy Kill* to the images of chaos that dominate *Blind Man with a*

Pistol is a powerful statement in itself concerning a crucial decade in American history.

But it is perhaps not so much what Himes says by way of protest as he extends the Grave Digger and Coffin Ed stories over the years that is important, but how he says it through the modification of the detective novel itself. He takes the view of life that is found in most detective stories and changes it considerably. The degree to which he does this can readily be seen in a consideration of the three views William O. Aydelotte in his article, "The Detective Story as a Historical Source," says are most commonly presented in detective novels. First, there is the idea that "In place of the complex issues of modern existence people in a detective story have very simple problems."[22] In most detective stories life goes on well except that a single crime, usually murder, has been committed. But in Himes's stories, all of the characters, even the most minor ones, have incredible problems because they are black and in Harlem. The complexities of the crimes that are under investigation, as bizarre as they always are, often are obscured by the complications in the life of a potential witness rousted from his bed in a tenement room by Grave Digger and Coffin Ed at four in the morning. Second, there is the point made by Aydelotte that "by other commonly used devices the detective story makes life more meaningful and endows the events it describes with significance, even with glamor.... In many subtle ways they help their readers to believe in the existence of a richer and fuller world."[23] Himes's Harlem is rich and his descriptions are exotic, but the overall impact is one of hellishness. The glamor is there, but it is glamor so fraught with danger and so often fueled by exploitation, degradation, and inhumanity that it hardly serves to make life seem more meaningful. Often the result is just the opposite. Himes seems to be inviting the question, can all of this chaos have meaning? And then there is Aydelotte's third contention, that "Finally, the detective story introduces us to a secure universe. We find here an ordered world obedient to fixed laws. The outcome is certain and the criminal will without fail be beaten by the detective. In this world man has power to control his own affairs and the problems of life can be mastered by human agency."[24] To a certain extent, this conception of order exists, although tenuously, in most of the Grave Digger and Coffin Ed stories. But, as we have seen, this is not the case in *Blind Man with a Pistol*. Here, amid scenes of riots that threaten the order of life in the United States itself, Himes eliminates the certain outcome and leaves the crimes unsolved. The detectives do not triumph over the criminal and we are introduced to a universe that is anything but secure.

This modification of the detective story is progressive and has a logic of its own that serves to vivify the explosive ending of *Blind Man with a Pistol*. The Harlem of Himes has often been seen as an inferno, and as the reader moves from one Grave Digger and Coffin Ed story to another, he moves from circle to circle. Order and reason are left farther and farther behind as the crimes Grave Digger and Coffin Ed must solve and the means of solution become ever more outrageous. Along with this progression, the Harlem inhabitants become increasingly grotesque until we come, finally, to Reverend Sam, his black clad wives, and his naked children. Harlem is blowing up, destroying itself as Grave Digger is calling Lieutenant Anderson about the blind man; but the apocalyptic scene is inevitable, given Himes's symbolic conception of his setting.

And Himes's Harlem is symbolic. It is not just that riots of the sort he describes did not happen in the

actual Harlem of the 1960s. And it is not just that his
Harlem geography is occasionally inexact. Harlem is
presented not only as representative of all the inner
cities of the United States, but also as an inner city of
the mind of white America. Harlem is black, isolated,
and repressed, but it is there and it must be dealt with.
Himes's images are frightening, much like the images
of the slaves in Melville's *Benito Cereno*, because they
relentlessly insist to white readers that something must
be done not with "the Negro Problem" but with the
white problem and the absurdities of racism.

It is this absurdity, by the way, that sometimes
makes Himes's characters, both black and white, appear as if they belong in cartoons instead of in a novel.
Himes's white cops often act like stereotypes of the
Irish flatfoot. And many of his blacks seem like caricatures right out of Amos and Andy. Himes has even
been accused of making his detective stories a series of
"nigger jokes."[25] But Himes's point is often missed—
the extremes of racism are so great in the United
States that what seems to be caricature is often real,
humorous, absurd and sad.

Nat Hentoff has written that "At base, Himes's
detective fiction is in the lean, crackling American
lineage of the experience-hardened balancer of evil
accounts who acts on the premise that a quick draw is
more utilitarian than a search warrant."[26] But because of the way he modifies the detective novel form,
Himes's Grave Digger and Coffin Ed stories represent
a considerable departure from the kind of crime fiction
readers have come to expect ever since the advent of
the hard-boiled detective in the 1920s.[27] Himes gives
the detective story added social purpose; and through
the creation of Grave Digger and Coffin Ed and the
depiction of the inner city in which they operate,
Himes rawly projects what it is like and what it means

to be black in America. In this sense he himself becomes a balancer of evil accounts and for white readers, at least, reading each of the Grave Digger and Coffin Ed books is like being presented with a search warrant. Search yourself, man.

The Strange Beauty
of Desperate Acts

"It's like Jazz; there's no inherent problem which prohibits understanding but the assumptions brought to it. . . . The understanding of art depends finally upon one's willingness to extend one's humanity and one's knowledge of human life."

—*Ralph Ellison*, "The Art of Fiction: An Interview"

Chester Himes's writing is predictable in perhaps one sense—it is always paced, as Nat Hentoff suggests in his review of *Cotton Comes to Harlem*, "like a hard-edged, up-tempo Charlie Parker blues."[1] But it is also writing that varies greatly in mood, Rabelaisian at one moment, bitterly serious and direct in another; and this makes for problems if one approaches Himes's books with too many assumptions. As we have seen, Himes progresses and changes incredibly in the course of his career, working his way through the urban realism of the Wright school, through assimilationism, through a confessional phase, and on into a discovery of the possibilities for art and social protest in the detective novel. All of his work, however, moves toward an extension of humanity and a shrewd knowledge of life in an America made absurd and literally driven crazy by racism; and his work demands that his readers be willing to make that same movement with him. The extent of this demand, and the range as well as the limits of Himes's artistry can be seen, by way of conclusion, through a look at his most atypical novel, a screenplay that was never filmed, and two apocalyptic short stories.

The novel is *Pinktoes*, a sexual farce first published by Olympia Press in Paris in 1961, and for a time Himes's best known novel in the United States. The novel's reputation was based partly on the rumor that it offers wildly explicit eroticism (a rumor that was greatly exaggerated) and its mockery of the pretensions and follies of American liberals, both black and white, who get caught up in the world of Mamie Mason, a Harlem hostess who promotes interracial sex as a means of solving racial problems and improving her own social status. This is Himes's only extended piece of satire and his "targets are the middle-class Negro who senses that the key to success is to think white and the white social reformer who thinks he must become black in order to solve the problem."[2] It is also a spoof of at least one aspect of the civil-rights movement and a self-parody of one of Himes's early and most persistent themes—the strange allure of white women for black men and black women for white men, a taboo that Himes exploits in a way that is hilarious and alleviating.

Pinktoes (the title derives from a sexual term used by blacks in reference to whites) begins with an introduction, "Excursion in Parodox," which features three prefatory fables (how Billie Hall fell and split her dress at the Copa, how a crew of porters had the last laugh on their white boss when asked to wash the street posts outside a new Horn and Hardart cafeteria in Manhattan on a cold night, and how a white cat and a black cat became friends in Harlem) that serve to demonstrate Himes's thesis that while everyone

agrees "Nothing ever goes right," human beings nonetheless furnish, through constant propagation of the
species, "the incontrovertible and absolute proof of our
faith in the fact that everything turns out as Some One
has planned it."[3] And where is the best example of this
faith to be found? Where else but in Harlem, explains
Himes in the opening chapter, "A Lesson in History":
"The people have faith. Why else would a forty-five
dollar a week porter go out on a Saturday night and
blow his whole pay on a pick-up in a bar? He's got
faith."[4] And who has the most faith? It is Mamie
Mason, the famous hostess, who wants "to serve the
Negro problem"[5] by serving blacks to whites and
whites to blacks at her carefully arranged parties.

After establishing Mamie's character by emphasizing her vanity (she lives on seeing her picture in the
social pages of the newspapers), her sexual preference
for white men, and the sometimes ludicrous results of
her constant dieting, Himes devotes most of the rest of
the novel to a description of one of Mamie's parties
and the amazing consequences the party has for two
of her guests: Wallace Wright, the great race leader
and Executive Chairman of the National Negro Political Society (NNPS); and Art Wills, an editor for a
publishing firm and soon to become the white managing editor of a proposed Negro picture magazine.

Mamie is angry at Wallace because he always
shows up at her parties without his wife, as if Mamie
is running a whorehouse instead of a salon. Through
complicated maneuvers, Mamie exposes Wallace's
affair with a white woman and the rumor gets started
that Wallace has left his middle-aged black wife, a
woman who had loyally stood by him through twenty
years of marriage, for a white woman half his age.
Racial pride suddenly comes to the rescue, with wom-
en's organizations adopting such slogans as "Be Happy

That You Are Nappy...Be Proud That You Are Black."[6] But at the same time, drugstores cannot stock enough hair-straightener and bleaching cream. Black historians counter by arguing that Cleopatra, the Queen of Sheba, Dido, Fatima, Aphrodite, and Eve were all black. Black poets write such poems as "The Whiter The Face The Blacker The Disgrace."[7] And this all goes to show, as Himes emphasizes, that the ladies of Harlem are not above losing their faith, as witnessed by the extremes to which they are willing to go in order to hang on to their men.

But it all has its counterpart as far as Art Wills is concerned. Mamie, out of anger with Art because he is apparently not going to feature her in the first issue of the picture magazine, lets his wife, Debbie, know that he had proposed marriage in a drunken letter to a black woman named Brown Sugar he had met at the party. Debbie goes home to her mother and word soon gets out that distinguished Negrophiles are leaving their long-suffering white wives for young brownskin beauties. There is an immediate run by white women on suntan lotions and ultra-violet ray lamps. A cosmetic firm that had been making a product called "Black Nomore" brings out a new product for whites called "Blackamoor." There is an accompanying rush by white women to kink their hair, dye their gums blue, and redden their eyes. And white women soon realize some of the advantages of being black, such as protection from sharks (it is well known that sharks dislike dark meat), being able to wear loud colors without being laughed at, and being able to hate all the blacks they want without feeling guilty.

Anthropologists, biologists, preachers, and physicists try to dispel the furor by arguing in various ways that there is no difference between the races and that the women should remain as they are; but neither side will listen—the women have too much faith. The result is an uproarious satire on the foibles of human sexuality and a parody of Himes's own idea of interracial sexual jealousy and curiosity as one source of the black-white conflict in the United States. On this point, Himes effectively reiterates what such social analysts as W. J. Cash and John Dollard have said concerning the sexual emotions behind lynchings, crossracial sexual aggression as an expression of supremacy, and the phobic fear of miscegenation that has provided a rationale for segregation.[8]

Himes's satire is not limited to black-white sexuality, however. Early in the book he describes a talk show involving two black writers, Edward Schooley and H. Randal Pine, co-authors of *Dreamland*, a book on drug addiction they had cribbed from an old WPA writers' project. Through the cocktail party staged before the show by the well-known editor Lou Reynolds, through the drunken discussion carried on during the show, and through the under-financed party staged afterwards in a midtown nightclub, Himes caricatures one aspect of the New York publishing scene in the 1950s.

Mamie's interracial party provides Himes with another opportunity for caricature when distinguished gentlemen meet to discuss some important matters. Some of the gentlemen include: Dr. Oliver Wendell Garrett, president of the board of directors of a foundation established by a Jewish philanthropist to promote love between blacks and southern whites; D. Stetson Kissock, head of the Southern Committee for the Preservation of Justice; Dr. Carl Vincent Stone, president emeritus of a famous deep south Negro college; Will Robbins, the white liberal movie producer (his latest film is entitled "Read and Run Nigger"); Lorenzo Llewellyn, forty-nine-years old and one of the

leading young black writers; and, of course, Wallace
Wright and Art Wills. The brilliant talk of these gentlemen includes remarks that "the Negro problem" is
all a matter of economics, that the answer lies in education, and that Jews have it far worse in Russia than
blacks have it in the United States. As the drinking
continues, the conversation shifts to a string of double
entendres involving chicken breasts, erecting images,
and soliciting members from all races. The party ends
with the guests pairing (and sometimes tripling) off to
engage in a variety of sexual practices that takes a
long chapter to describe. Included along with this description are several side stories featuring, for example,
Panama Paul's dream of being in a heaven full of
white angels but being unable to fly because his testicles are weighted down with anvils, and Reverend
Riddick's buck-naked wrestling match with a demon-
possessed husband and wife.

In an important way, *Pinktoes* thus provides welcome relief from the sometimes overwhelmingly bitter
and deadly serious literature that deals with the character types and themes Himes simply pokes fun at.
The novel is, of course, a vicious attack, as most satire
of its type is, on people and activities Himes has little
stomach for and even less patience. And at times the
humor in the novel is anything but light, as at least
one reviewer pointed out: "This allegedly Rabelaisian
romp in and around Harlem . . . has the levity of a
jackhammer."[9] But Himes's jackhammer does serve to
break up the rigid literary forms in which the topics of
Pinktoes are usually discussed, although the book does
have its deficiencies. It has too large a cast of characters (by the end, however, they are surprisingly well
sorted out), the transitions as in so many of Himes's
other novels are not always smooth, and there are so
many asides and tangential episodes that the work

takes on the qualities of a shaggy-dog story. But the overall effect of *Pinktoes* is to show something not always apparent in much of Himes's earlier work, that he "is a superb humorist and has complete mastery of his material. . . . Beyond being rowdy, boisterous, and utterly delightful, *Pinktoes* encourages a more realistic look at social inequities and perhaps more carefully measured strides toward total civil rights."[10]

Himes's realistic look at inequities takes the form of quite a different vision in a work that shows another side of him and indicates, despite its ultimate failure, the breadth of his artistic range. *Baby Sister* was written at the suggestion of European producers who considered the film version of Lorraine Hansberry's *Raisin in the Sun* a failure and suggested that Himes deal with the same material—the problems of family life amid the conditions of Harlem—but avoid the unrealistic and aesthetically unacceptable idealism and the happy ending of Hansberry's play. So, in 1961 in a one-room penthouse in the "old town" of Antibes, Himes set to work. "As the story of Baby Sister unfolded in my mind," he later wrote, "I was moved to tears. When not crying I was singing at the top of my voice: *What did I do to be so black and blue?*"[11]

The scenario begins with a voice-over as the camera pans the Harlem streets: "This is Harlem, U.S.A., a city of contradictions. A city of Negroes isolated in the center of New York City. A city of incredible poverty and huge sums of cash. . . ."[12] Baby Sister Louis is a beautiful and sensuous seventeen-year-old who lives with her mother and three brothers, Susie (twenty-two), Buddy (twenty), and Pigmeat (fourteen). Her older sister, Lil, is a blues singer. The family lives in an area of Harlem known as The Valley, where Baby Sister has little chance for survival among the hungry wolves and those who are trying to save

themselves from the wolves. Her father has already
been killed defending her honor and her youngest
brother appears to be next as he stands throwing rocks
at the car of Slick Collins, a pimp who wants to make
Baby Sister his "side piece." Baby Sister runs to the
Church of the Redeemed Sinner where her father's
funeral is taking place and tells her older brothers that
Slick is going after Pigmeat with a knife. Susie corners
Slick, knocks him down, and makes him swear that he
will leave her alone.

When Baby Sister and her brothers get back to
the church, their father's body is being loaded into the
hearse, but Baby Sister refuses to go to the graveyard.
Instead, she walks to 116th Street midway between
Lenox and Seventh Avenues where the two plain-
clothes detectives, one white and one black, who have
been assigned to investigate her father's murder are
talking in their car. When they see Baby Sister approach, the black detective gets out and walks away.
Baby Sister gets into the car with the white detective,
Lieutenant Fischer, with whom, it is soon apparent,
she has been having an affair. What is more, she is
pregnant. Fischer promises to take her to an abortion-
ist the next day, then drives her to Blumstein's Department Store where he gives her money to buy a yellow
dress.

She takes the dress to Lil's apartment, where she
admits that Fischer bought it for her. Lil reminds her
that her brothers would kill her if they knew she was
involved with a white detective. As she walks home,
nearly every man she meets accosts her and she has to
fend off or ignore one proposition after another. When
she finally gets home, Susie rips open the package the
dress is in and chases her out. She escapes by getting
into a car with a stranger and winds up, after a reefer
party, after a session at the Renaissance Ballroom, and

after whiskey highballs and chicken at the Chicken
Shack, at the storefront church of her mother's
preacher, the Reverend Converted Sinner, so she will
have an alibi to get back into the apartment. But even
the preacher tries to rape her. She runs home but is
attacked by a man on the stairway. She escapes by
biting his hand, slashing out with her knife, and
screaming.

The next day we see Susie and Slick in a barber
shop discussing a deal. Susie has agreed to sell Baby
Sister to Slick for $5,000. We notice that there is a
bandage across the palm of Susie's hand. Slick says he
is having trouble raising the money. Susie says that if
he does not come up with it soon, he will sell her
downtown because she is easily a $100 whore. Fischer,
who has heard about the attempted rape, and his
partner enter the barber shop and ask where Susie was
the night before. Fischer sees the bandage and knocks
Susie from the chair with a pistol. Fischer walks out
telling Susie that if Baby Sister names him as her as-
sailant, it is all over for him.

Lil, meanwhile, has talked her man, Dickie, a sax-
ophone player, into getting Baby Sister on the Apollo
Amateur Hour. Fischer, when he learns of Baby Sister's appearance, tells her that he will give her $100 if
she wins and that he will be waiting for her outside
her apartment during the after-performance party her
mother has scheduled. Slick, who realizes that his
chances of getting Baby Sister are rapidly diminishing,
tells Pigmeat that Fischer has made Baby Sister his
mistress and that he plans to take her away after the
contest. Pigmeat vows to kill Fischer and steals a .38-
caliber revolver from Slick's car to do it.

The next scene is the Apollo Theatre. The Master
of Ceremonies announces that the first prize for the
winning vocalist is a recording session with Universal

Records and a week's engagement with a name band. Dickie has arranged to get Baby Sister on last, and when she appears, the audience goes wild. She wins easily and seems to be on the verge of escaping from the violence and degradation that have surrounded her all her life.

Back at the party, Susie is disconsolate. He knows that he has lost out and so has Slick. Midway through the celebration, Baby Sister runs down to look for Fischer. Pigmeat tries to stop her but she gets around him and dashes toward the police car. Pigmeat starts shooting. Fischer instinctively puts three bullets through his shattered windshield and knocks Pigmeat down. Susie, hearing the shots, dashes down the stairs, pulls out a knife, and runs at Fischer. The detective fires twice but does not stop Susie, who lunges ahead and stabs him in the heart.

The final scene is another funeral at the Church of the Redeemed Sinner. The coffins of Pigmeat and Susie are up front. Unable to control herself, Baby Sister flees during the middle of the service. The Reverend Converted Sinner orders the congregation to chase her. Buddy catches up with her first, then the congregation gathers around and, chorus-like, condemns her.

Baby Sister is a Greek tragedy of sorts with its twin themes of incest and the family-curse; and it is a starkly moving depiction of family life in Harlem. As a scenario it makes use of the potential of film to leave powerful and disturbing images—the two funerals, Baby Sister trying to walk home while being accosted, the reefer party and the ballroom, and the contest at the Apollo—hanging in the mind. The problem with it is that it errors in the opposite direction of *A Raisin in the Sun*—it is too stark, too negative. Even though the conditions in Harlem may be as terrible as Himes indicates they are, *Baby Sister*, because of its relentless anger, its unalloyed determinism, and its narrow range of hopefulness (is there indeed no other escape for Baby Sister than to win a contest at the Apollo?), fails in the end to convince. But it is a work of considerable impact nonetheless, not so much for its story line as for its attempt at capturing a kind of despair that permeates the black side of racial conditions in the United States much more than does the optimism of Lorraine Hansberry.

This despair, along with a grim consideration of some solutions to the problems handled so playfully in *Pinktoes* and so unplayfully in *Baby Sister*, finds a voice of another sort in two short stories published by Himes in the late 1960s.

"Tang" (1967) opens with T-bone Smith sitting in his cold-water flat watching television with his wife, Tang. T-bone is broke, unemployed, and is trying to talk Tang into going to Central Park to pick up a man so they will have some money to buy food. The doorbell rings and a messenger leaves a long package, tied with a red ribbon, for T-bone. He and Tang think at first that the package holds flowers, but that makes no sense. Who would send flowers to T-bone? It turns out to be an M-14 rifle along with a note instructing T-bone to learn his weapon because freedom is near. Tang is excited—she knows that it is the uprising. T-bone is terrified and starts out to get the cops. Tang picks up the rifle and tells him that if he makes one move for the police she will shoot. He grabs at her and she pulls the trigger, but the rifle is not loaded. He slashes her with his knife as she screams, "I shoulda known, you are whitey's slave; you'll never be free."[13]

"Prediction" (1969) begins with a parade being held in an unnamed large American city to demon-

strate the power of the police during a time of aggra-
vated suspicion between the races. No black policemen are taking part in the march and only whites are
watching. One black man is present, however; he is
waiting inside the front door of the Catholic cathedral
on Main Street. He sits straddling the collection box
and looks out through the slots where the donations
are dropped. He has an automatic rifle. "He sat patiently, as though he had all the time in the world,
waiting for the parade to come into sight," Himes
writes. "He had all the remainder of his life. Subjec-
tively, he had waited four hundred years for this moment and he was not in a hurry. The parade would
come, he knew, and he would be waiting for it."[14]
What he is doing he knows he must do alone, in the
hope that it will make life safer for his race in the
future. When he begins to fire, a horrible scene of
carnage results, certainly the most gruesome in all of
Himes's scenes—faces explode, brains are sprayed on
the street, jawbones are unhinged. Before the sniper is
blasted into a few shreds of black skin by a riot tank,
he kills forty-seven policemen, two hundred and
twenty-six white bystanders, and wounds another
seventy-five. The stock market collapses, the dollar
falls, and the capitalistic system begins to fail. The
story ends with two words, "Good night."[15]

This story—written, says Himes, after he "had be-
come fully convinced that the only chance Black
Americans had of attaining justice and equality in the
United States of America was by violence,"[16]—along
with "Tang," points to a concern that runs all through
Himes's work, including *Pinktoes* and *Baby Sister*, a
concern with solutions to the plight of his characters.
The plight on one hand is seen in social terms and here
Himes's pervasive despair, whether it is expressed

through satire or not, takes over. For Baby Sister as well as for Bob Jones in *If He Hollers Let Him Go*, there is no solution within the system. Interracial parties may be held, revolutions may be planned, but none of it will work. Greed, lust, and sheer cowardice will always get in the way. Black women like Tang may have faith, may pick up the M-14, but the T-bones are too morally and physically exhausted to do any more than they have always done. But on the other hand, the plight is seen in existential terms, and here Himes expresses a vision that, despite the hideous scenes that often accompany it, is transcendent. It is this vision that enables the hero of "Prediction" (who experiences "spiritual ecstasy"[17] as he sees his white targets fall and thinks of all the humiliation he and his people have suffered) to exert himself existentially like Lee Gordon and Grave Digger and Coffin Ed against overwhelming odds. The images here are ones of incredible violence, but the underlying ideas are, paradoxically, ennobling and heroic given the world of, say, *Baby Sister* where the only conditions of life are ignobility and cowardice.

But whatever vision Himes chooses to express, his writing is icily incisive in its penetration of the American racial scene, so incisive that he is often frightening in his ability to evoke the terror of situations from which there is no exit other than desperation. But then he is also able to evoke the strange beauty inherent in desperate acts. What T. M. Curran wrote of *Black on Black* certainly holds for all of Himes's major work: "[These] writings are powerful and, indeed, bear the authentic impress of a master. Himes is in absolute control of all moods and all forms. He can be tragic or hilariously funny, poignantly ironic or savagely vicious, absurd or coldly logical."[18] But it is more than his range that makes Himes unique; there is no other writer like him because he is hard-edged and up-tempo, a rule unto himself—articulate, durable to the point where even his failures are impressive, and always making the disturbing demands upon his readers that only mastery of form permits.

Notes

NOVEMBER 1928

1. For this aspect of his life see Chester Himes, *The Quality of Hurt: The Autobiography of Chester Himes* (Garden City: Doubleday, 1972), I, 47–59.
2. *The Quality of Hurt*, p. 101.
3. *The Quality of Hurt*, p. 36.
4. *The Quality of Hurt*, pp. 65–66.
5. *The Quality of Hurt*, p. 73.
6. John A. Williams, *Flashbacks: A Twenty-Year Diary of Article Writing* (Garden City: Anchor Press/Doubleday, 1974), p. 321.
7. Williams, p. 322.
8. W. S. Lynch, rev. of *If He Hollers Let Him Go*, by Chester Himes, *Saturday Review*, 17 Nov. 1945, p. 53.
9. Chester Himes, "Author Talks Back," *Saturday Review*, 28 Nov. 1945, p. 50.
10. Williams, p. 303.
11. Robert Bone, *The Negro Novel in America* (New Haven and London: Yale University Press, 1965), p. 115.
12. Williams, pp. 304–305.
13. Chester Himes, "Dilemma of the Negro Novelist in the United States," in *Beyond the Angry Black*, ed. John A. Williams (New York: Cooper Square, 1966), pp. 51–58.

14. "Dilemma of the Negro Novelist in the United States," p. 53.
15. "Dilemma of the Negro Novelist in the United States," p. 53.
16. "Dilemma of the Negro Novelist in the United States, p. 54.
17. "Dilemma of the Negro Novelist in the United States," p. 55.
18. "Dilemma of the Negro Novelist in the United States," p. 56.
19. "Dilemma of the Negro Novelist in the United States," p. 57.
20. *The Quality of Hurt*, p. 115.
21. *The Quality of Hurt*, p. 141.
22. *The Quality of Hurt*, p. 224.

TWO WAR NOVELS

1. Robert Bone, *The Negro Novel in America* (New Haven and London: Yale University Press, 1965), p. 156.
2. Bone, p. 158.
3. Edward Margolies, *Native Sons: A Critical Study of Twentieth-Century Negro American Authors* (Philadelphia and New York: J. P. Lippincott Company, 1968), p. 88.
4. Margolies, p. 90.
5. Chester Himes, *If He Hollers Let Him Go*, Signet edition (New York: New American Library, 1971), p. 7.
6. *If He Hollers Let Him Go*, p. 14.
7. *If He Hollers Let Him Go*, p. 37.
8. Joseph Warren Beach, rev. of *If He Hollers Let Him Go*, by Chester Himes, *New York Times*, 2 Dec. 1945, p. 7.
9. *If He Hollers Let Him Go*, p. 73.
10. *If He Hollers Let Him Go*, p. 88.
11. *If He Hollers Let Him Go*, p. 116.

12. *If He Hollers Let Him Go*, p. 116.
13. *If He Hollers Let Him Go*, p. 138.
14. *If He Hollers Let Him Go*, p. 142.
15. *If He Hollers Let Him Go*, p. 144.
16. *If He Hollers Let Him Go*, p. 175.
17. *If He Hollers Let Him Go*, p. 186.
18. *If He Hollers Let Him Go*, p. 191.
19. Rev. of *If He Hollers Let Him Go*, by Chester Himes, *Weekly Book Review* 4 Nov. 1945, p. 10.
20. *If He Hollers Let Him Go*, p. 8.
21. Bone, p. 144.
22. Bone, p. 115.
23. Richard Wright, "I Tried to Be a Communist," *Atlantic Monthly* (Aug. 1944), p. 62.
24. Wilson Record, *The Negro and the Communist Party* (Chapel Hill: University of North Carolina Press, 1951), p. 110.
25. Walter Rideout, *The Radical Novel in the United States, 1900–1954* (Cambridge: Harvard University Press, 1956), p. 67.
26. Chester Himes, *Lonely Crusade* (New York: Knopf, 1947), p. 17.
27. *Lonely Crusade*, p. 24.
28. *Lonely Crusade*, p. 34.
29. *Lonely Crusade*, p. 46.
30. *Lonely Crusade*, p. 61.
31. *Lonely Crusade*, p. 70.
32. *Lonely Crusade*, p. 106.
33. *Lonely Crusade*, p. 161.
34. *Lonely Crusade*, p. 188.
35. *Lonely Crusade*, p. 328.
36. *Lonely Crusade*, p. 361.
37. *Lonely Crusade*, p. 383.
38. *Lonely Crusade*, p. 386.
39. Stowan Christowe, rev. of *Lonely Crusade*, by Chester Himes, *Atlantic Monthly*, Oct. 1947, p. 138.
40. Rev. of *Lonely Crusade*, by Chester Himes, *New Yorker*, 13 Sept. 1947, p. 120.

41. George Streator, rev. of *Lonely Crusade,* by Chester
     Himes, *Commonweal,* 3 Oct. 1947, p. 604.
41. Streator, p. 604.

"SOMETHING TO HATE ME FOR":
THE CONFESSIONAL NOVELS

1.   Robert Bone, *The Negro Novel in America* (New
     Haven and London: Yale University Press, 1965),
     p. 168.
2.   Chester Himes, *Cast the First Stone,* Signet edition
     (New York: New American Library, 1972), p. 53.
3.   *Cast the First Stone,* p. 41.
4.   *Cast the First Stone,* p. 219.
5.   *Cast the First Stone,* pp. 300–301.
6.   *Cast the First Stone,* p. 303.
7.   W. R. Burnett, rev. of *Cast the First Stone,* by Ches-
     ter Himes, *Saturday Review,* 17 Jan. 1953, p. 15.
8.   Frederic Morton, rev. of *Cast the First Stone,* by
     Chester Himes, *New York Herald Tribune Book Re-
     view,* 18 Jan. 1953, p. 8.
9.   Chester Himes, *The Third Generation,* Signet edi-
     tion (New York: New American Library, 1956), p.
     11.
10. *The Third Generation,* pp. 131–32.
11. *The Third Generation,* p. 196.
12. *The Third Generation,* p. 316.
13. David Littlejohn, *Black on White: A Critical Survey
     of Writing by American Negroes* (New York: Gross-
     man, 1966), p. 143.
14. Riley Hughes, rev. of *The Third Generation,* by
     Chester Himes, *Catholic World,* April 1954, p. 72.
15. Edmund Fuller, rev. of *The Third Generation,* by
     Chester Himes, *Chicago Sunday Tribune,* 10 Jan.
     1954, p. 5.
16. John Brooks, rev. of *The Third Generation,* by Ches-
     ter Himes, *New York Times,* 10 Jan. 1954, p. 29.

17. Chester Himes, *The Primitive*, Signet edition (New York: New American Library, 1955), p. 14.
18. *The Primitive*, p. 22.
19. *The Primitive*, p. 52.
20. *The Primitive*, p. 67.
21. *The Primitive*, p. 71.
22. *The Primitive*, p. 101.
23. *The Primitive*, pp. 101–102.
24. *The Primitive*, p. 105.
25. *The Primitive*, p. 137.
26. *The Primitive*, p. 158.
27. *The Primitive*, p. 158.
28. *The Primitive*, p. 159.
29. Edward Margolies, *Native Sons: A Critical Study of Twentieth-Century Negro American Authors* (Philadelphia and New York: J. P. Lippincott Company, 1968), p. 93.
30. Chester Himes, *The Quality of Hurt: The Autobiography of Chester Himes* (Garden City: Doubleday, 1972), I, p. 301.
31. *The Primitive*, p. 160.

SEARCH WARRANTS FOR THE INNER CITY

1. Shane Stevens, rev. of *Blind Man with a Pistol*, by Chester Himes, *Book World*, 27 April 1969, p. 4.
2. Philip Durham, "The 'Black Mask' School" in *Tough Guy Writers of the Thirties*, ed. David Madden (Carbondale and Edwardsville: Southern Illinois University Press, 1968), p. 51.
3. Herbert Ruhm, "Raymond Chandler: From Bloomsbury to the Jungle—and Beyond," in *Tough Guy Writers of the Thirties*, p. 176.
4. Chester Himes, *Cotton Comes to Harlem* (New York: Putnam, 1965), p. 18.
5. *Cotton Comes to Harlem*, p. 20.
6. Chester Himes, *The Crazy Kill* (New York: Berkeley, 1959), p. 33.

7.   *The Crazy Kill*, p. 33.

8.   *The Crazy Kill*, pp. 78–79.

9.   Stevens, p. 4.

10. Chester Himes, "Preface," *Blind Man with a Pistol*
     (New York: Morrow, 1969).

11. *Blind Man with a Pistol*, p. 22.

12. *Blind Man with a Pistol*, p. 55.

13. *Blind Man with a Pistol*, p. 102.

14. *Blind Man with a Pistol*, p. 193.

15. *Blind Man with a Pistol*, p. 194.

16. Edward Margolies, rev. of *Blind Man with a Pistol*,
     by Chester Himes, *Saturday Review*, 22 March 1969,
     p. 64.

17. *Blind Man with a Pistol*, p. 218.

18. *Blind Man with a Pistol*, p. 221.

19. *Blind Man with a Pistol*, p. 215.

20. *Blind Man with a Pistol*, p. 215.

21. Ross Macdonald, "The Writer as Detective Hero," in
     The Mystery Writer's Art, ed. Francis M. Nevins, Jr.
     (Bowling Green, Ohio: Bowling Green University
     Press, 1970), pp. 295–96.

22. Willam O. Aydelotte, "The Detective Story as His-
     torical Source" in *The Mystery Writer's Art*, p. 309.

23. Aydelotte, p. 310.

24. Aydelotte, p. 311.

25. Margolies, p. 65.

26. Nat Hentoff, rev. of *Cotton Comes to Harlem*, by
     Chester Himes, *Book Week*, 28 March 1965, p. 11.

27. For a different but valuable treatment of Himes's
     detective stories, see Edward Margolies, "The Thril-
     lers of Chester Himes," *Studies in Black Literature*,
     I, ii (1970), 1–11.

THE STRANGE BEAUTY OF DESPERATE ACTS

1.   Nat Hentoff, rev. of *Cotton Comes to Harlem*, by
     Chester Himes, *Book Week*, 28 March 1965, p. 11.

2. J.L.S., rev. of *Pinktoes*, by Chester Himes, *Best Sellers*, 15 July 1965, p. 171.

3. Chester Himes, *Pinktoes* (Covina, Cal.: Collectors Publications, 1968), p. 1.

4. *Pinktoes*, p. 21.

5. *Pinktoes*, p. 23.

6. *Pinktoes*, p. 130.

7. *Pinktoes*, p. 131.

8. For more information on this point, see Francis E. Kearns's introduction to *The Black Experience*, ed. Francis E. Kearns (New York: Viking, 1970), pp. xv–xvii.

9. Martin Levin, rev. of *Pinktoes*, by Chester Himes, *New York Times Book Review*, 15 August 1965, p. 30.

10. J.L.S., p. 171.

11. Chester Himes, *Black on Black; Baby Sister and Selected Writings* (Garden City: Doubleday, 1973), p. 7.

12. *Black on Black*, p. 11.

13. *Black on Black*, p. 138.

14. *Black on Black*, p. 282.

15. *Black on Black*, p. 287.

16. *Black on Black*, pp. 7–8.

17. *Black on Black*, p. 286.

18. T. M. Curran, rev. of *Black on Black*, by Chester Himes, *America*, 21 July 1973, p. 44.

Bibliography

1. WORKS BY CHESTER HIMES

NOVELS

If He Hollers Let Him Go. Garden City: Doubleday, 1945.
Lonely Crusade. New York: Knopf, 1947.
Cast the First Stone. New York: Coward McCann, 1952.
The Third Generation. Cleveland: World, 1954.
The Primitive. New York: New American Library, 1955.
For Love of Imabelle. New York: Fawcett, 1957.
The Crazy Kill. New York: Berkeley, 1959.
Real Cool Killers. New York: Berkeley, 1959.
All Shot Up. New York: Berkeley, 1960.
The Big Gold Dream. New York: Berkeley, 1960.
Pinktoes. Paris: Olympia Press, 1961; New York: Putnam, 1965; New York: Stein and Day, 1965.
Cotton Comes to Harlem. New York: Putnam, 1965.
A Rage in Harlem (reprint of *For Love of Imabelle*). New York: Avon, 1965.
The Heat's On. New York: Putnam, 1966.
Run Man Run. New York: Putnam, 1966.
Blind Man with a Pistol. New York: Morrow, 1969.
Hot Day, Hot Night. New York: Morrow, 1971.

COLLECTED WRITINGS:
SCREENPLAYS, ESSAYS, SHORT STORIES

Black on Black; Baby Sister and Selected Writings. Garden City: Doubleday, 1973.

AUTOBIOGRAPHY

The Quality of Hurt: The Autobiography of Chester Himes.
Volume I. Garden City: Doubleday, 1973.

2. WORKS ABOUT CHESTER HIMES

Bakish, David. "Chester Himes." *Encyclopedia of World
    Literature in the Twentieth Century.* IV. New York:
    Frederick Ungar Publishing Co., 1975, pp. 159–161.
Bone, Robert. *The Negro Novel in America.* New Haven
    and London: Yale University Press, 1965, pp. 157–76.
Chelminski, R. "Hard-Bitten Old Pro." *Life* (28 August
    1970): 60–61.
Hughes, Carl Milton. *The Negro Novelist: A Discussion of
    the Writings of American Negro Novelists, 1940–1950.*
    New York: Citadel Press, 1953, pp. 206–12.
Littlejohn, David. *Black on White: A Critical Survey of
    Writing by American Negroes.* New York: Grossman,
    1966, pp. 142–43.
Margolies, Edward. *Native Sons: A Critical Study of Twen-
    tieth-Century Negro American Authors.* Philadelphia
    and New York: J. B. Lippincott Company, 1968, pp.
    87–101.
————. "The Thrillers of Chester Himes." *Studies in Black
    Literature.* I, ii (1970): 1–11.
Micha, René. "Les paroissiens de Chester Himes." *Temps
    Modernes.* XX (1965), 1507–23.
"PW Interviews." *Publishers Weekly* (3 April 1972).
Williams, John A. "My Man Himes." *Flashbacks: A
    Twenty-Year Diary of Article Writing.* Garden City:
    Anchor Press/Doubleday, 1974, pp. 292–352.
Special Himes issue, *Black Writers* (March 1972).

Index